ARISE ZOMBIE NATION

ARISE ZOMBIE NATION

Awake To A Passionate Life

Shelley Sharpe

Sister With a Flashlight, LLC.

Spokane, Washington

Arise Zombie Nation © Shelley Kennedy-Sharpe. All Rights Reserved, except where otherwise noted.

CONTENTS

Permissions and Copyright Page   vii
Gratitude and Acknowledgements   ix
Praise for Contributions   xi
Preface   xiii
Introduction   1
Awake to a Passionate Life
Shelley Kennedy-Sharpe

1. Have You Been Bitten?   7
2. Awake to a Passionate Life!   17
3. The Battle for Your Soul   25
4. Blood, Bone, Heart, and Brain   33
5. Calling All Angels   41
6. Trekking to the New Jerusalem   51
7. Aligning With The Stars   61
8. Breath Of Life   67
9. The Way of the Master   75
10. The Light on the Hill, Hades, Jupiter, the Earth, and the Moon   81
11. The Past, the Future and the Quantum Mechanics of Now   89
12. Speaking the World into Being   97
13. Lost, Found and Given   107
14. Sitting in Holiness, Resting in Mercy   113

References Cited	121
Body and Mind Extended Bibliography	125
Spirit Extended Bibliography	128
Scripture References	133
Afterward	144
Authors Note	

PERMISSIONS AND COPYRIGHT PAGE

Arise Zombie Nation: Awake to a Passionate Life, Shelley Sharpe Copyright © 2015 All rights reserved. Published 2016, by Sister with a Flashlight, LLC. Spokane, Washington. 99206 All rights reserved.

Cover design (c) Sister With a Flashlight, LLC. All rights reserved.

Scripture quotations taken from the 21st Century King James Version®, copyright © 1994. Used by permission of Deuel Enterprises, Inc., Gary, SD 57237. All rights reserved.

Scripture quotations taken from the Amplified® Bible, Copyright © 1954, 1958, 1962, 1964, 1965, 1987 by The Lockman Foundation Used by permission." (www.Lockman.org)

Scripture taken from the HOLY BIBLE, NEW INTERNATIONAL VERSION®. Copyright © 1973, 1978, 1984 Biblica. Used by permission of Zondervan. All rights reserved.

The "NIV" and "New International Version" trademarks are registered in the United States Patent and Trademark

Office by Biblica. Use of either trademark requires the permission of Biblica.

Scripture quotations marked (NLT) are taken from the Holy Bible, New Living Translation, copyright © 1996, 2004, 2007 by Tyndale House Foundation. Used by permission of Tyndale House Publishers, Inc., Carol Stream, IL 60188. All rights reserved.

GRATITUDE AND ACKNOWLEDGEMENTS

To my husband Paul Sharpe, thank you for your encouragement and sacrifice during the writing and editing of this book. You never made me feel guilty!

To my children Jessica Sharpe and Trevor Sharpe, thank you for teaching me more about love than I could ever have dreamed.

To my mentors:
Jesus Christ, the LOVE of my life, I sing your praises.

Michael Bennett, Sandra Vesterstein, of Bennett Stellar University. Thank you for your curriculum, your humanity, your thought leadership, and your faithful and tireless work helping to heal the world!

Mark and Magali Peysha, thank you for your training and your brilliant, integrative coaching strategies that were presented at the Strategic Intervention Camp. I have been honored to be present at your events and have been changed by you and all of the people attending. Each time has been life changing.

To my friends:
Deborah Lilly Coupey, thank you for helping me sort through structure and concepts and for always encouraging me to stretch, dream, and weave it all together.

Stephanie Ericksen, thank you for being present for it all, hearing my first words, my first thoughts, the first chapter and being a great cheerleader.

Lynn Vincent, thank you for believing in my visions, my journey and for being a lifelong friend.

To so many family members and friends who have *suffered* me talking about this-you are all dearly loved and I am very grateful for your kindness.

PRAISE FOR CONTRIBUTIONS

There were two people that helped me to publish a better book. An artist and fellow life coach- Isabelle Guilbert and final editor Jacque Leonard both will forever have my gratitude.

To Isabelle Guilbert, Thank you for helping me realize exactly what I wanted and what I did not want for my cover art. Helping me to clarify my vision was a gift. We learned a great deal together.

To Jacque Leonard, my final editor and proofreader, thank you for your patience and for helping me to *craft* better sentences that do not change the content or the meaning. Getting to know you better was a true, unexpected gift. Thank you!

PREFACE

Some people will not think that this book is "Christian enough." Some will say it is not "inclusive enough." I ask you to lay down all your judgements and allow for discernment as you read. You can sift the chaff from the grain to use what you need and what makes you stronger. Many scriptures convey beautiful truths and useful wisdom. See what you can connect and align with your core values. I am not suggesting that if you are a Christian you should throw out discernment. Rather, I am asking you to suspend judgment until you have read the entire book and have checked all of it with the Word and the Holy Spirit. For those of you who hold the tenants of other faiths, please do the same-check it with the tenants of your faith or belief system. See if there is anything good, lovely or honorable in the pages of this book then keep them and keep the learning. Also, feel free to throw out the rest. I present only an opportunity to learn more about yourself and what you believe.

INTRODUCTION

AWAKE TO A PASSIONATE LIFE

SHELLEY KENNEDY-SHARPE

Over the past several years, I became fascinated with the cultural draw towards Zombies. I was shocked by the numbers of new movies and television shows featuring the walking dead, the rising dead, the armies of dead. I began asking young people why they liked these shows and what they found so compelling. After formulating a theory in my mind, I forgot about it.

In September of 2015, I took a long vacation to Rome, the Greek Islands, and Ephesus, Turkey. When the cruise ship docked in Turkey, I took a tour to the home of Jesus' mother, Mary, the home that John built for her. It was at the top of a mountain in Ephesus. I was so excited to be where Jesus, John, Mary, and later Paul had walked. I thought of their steps as I walked the path to the fountains. These fountains were made from the springs where Mary drank. The Pope of Rome declared Mary's small two-room home a Holy pilgrimage sight. The water from the springs was declared to be Holy as well. I filled my water bottle from the fountain; I drank it down and refilled. The tour company gave me a small clay jug to fill as a gift; I filled that as well. When I drank the water, I knew something was different. I felt I could see and hear more clearly. I prayed that further changes would be revealed to me. I prayed that the water had changed every part of my being.

When I arrived home to the U.S.A., it was a Saturday evening. I went to church on the following Thursday. When I came home from church, I looked at the picture on my calendar and I read the caption. It said "Do what God says to do." It was a Kenneth Copeland Ministries calendar. I asked, "Okay, Lord what would you have me do?" Then, as I had learned to do, I sat down with pen and paper to listen and take notes. When I looked up, twenty minutes later, I saw that I had written down the name of this book and fourteen chapter heads. Mary's water *had* made me hear more clearly! I believe that I was called to write this. I am not saying that I did my job well. Rather I allowed my mind and fingers to be used to complete this given task with the best skills and attention I possessed.

You might be asking, "Why you?" I asked myself the same question. As I wrote this book, I became aware of why I was uniquely prepared to write "Arise Zombie Nation, Awake to a Passionate Life." It became clear that I knew more than I believed about the topics. At first, when I read the Chapter titles, I said, "I know nothing about that!" But, each time I started a new chapter the words would fly onto the page. As time went by, I saw that my whole life had been a preparation for writing this book. I saw that the trials, traumas, dramas, and torments of my life had lead to incredible learning. I flashed on the thousands of books I have read since I was eleven years old. All were seeds, soil, water, and sun that led to this harvest.

All of the trials and tribulations that my family and I had endured were training camps for the future-Now. We had suffered 11 losses of family members in 18 months. Long periods of illnesses and injuries were worse than the deaths. My mother was paralyzed, then she subsequently died of a blood clot. My father died after a long battle with cancer. My father-in-law died in our home after five-year battle with another type of cancer, Melanoma. My brother died when a brain shunt became clogged and blew up his heart. My daughter was in a car accident that changed her body forever. She endured 17 broken bones, 7 rods, 7 plates, 37 screws. Also, 8 percent of her body was burned by battery acid and the engine that ended up being pushed onto her lap, burning her left leg to the bone. She lost a large part of her left thigh from what they call a "de-gloving injury."

I am very grateful for my daughter's amazing will and passion to keep moving. Fully clothed -neck to toe- you would not be able to see any damage. She walks and runs and out runs every limitation that the experts insisted she would have. She ended up having fourteen surgeries and was not expected to keep her left leg. Our faith, her courage, our words, her work, His Love, and Grace became the ingredients for an inspirational story of a miraculous magnitude. Words have the power to change things. His Word has the power over all things.

During these trials, The Word of God was a treasure hidden in my heart and it was what sustained me during these difficult times. I saw how speaking the "Word," over the lives of the people in our family, changed them and me. I found that I could lean into the Word and focus on the beauty, strength, courage and the power of words. I learned during worship that words, like rain, fall on the believer and nonbeliever alike. I learned that gravity works on us all and that certain principles have been built into the very fabric of life! These principles work whether we believe in them or not. Things we cannot see are still at work every day to bless us and keep us. Gravity keeps us attached to this earth and the heavens in place. Rain makes everything grow. Oxygen is an unseen, but critical, aspect of life.

In 2011, after my daughter's horrific accident, I decided to learn everything I could about how words affect not only our brains but all living things. I studied great minds, orators, teachers, preachers, Wisemen and ancient texts. I became certified by Bennett Stellar in Mind, Body and Spirit Healing. I received certificates in Neuro-linguistic Programing, Reiki, Hypnosis, Timeline, and Life Coaching. I studied under Mark and Magali Peysha to learn Strategic Intervention strategies. I then worked at creating my own method of combining all the learning and all of the techniques. I studied brain science and the use of "mirror neurons." I researched how words can create new Neuro-pathways and how the brain can heal itself.

I did not know that all of this life and learning was going to take the shape and form it has. I did not understand that all of the various threads of interests, which looked like an eclectic mess when I was younger, would turn into a beautiful tapestry on this side of my life. But, everything that I have done in the past has led me to understand where I am and how I got here. It has taught me how to get out of the swamp and how to walk out of a nightmare. It showed me the way to rise up to a new and passionate life. I found my Path!

This book is my desire to be a *sister with a flashlight* to show you how to find your *Passionate Life*. You may have never been a *Zombie*. You may have been just asleep, but now you can take this journey into discovering "You!" Can you hear the song of your soul crying out to you? This book will help you gather your missing notes and "materialize" your original design and purpose! I pray this book helps you find more of what you love, what makes you strong, and what helps to illuminate who you are! I hope you see how you can use "Everything" all the bad and the good to propel you towards YOUR Passionate Life!

Chapter 1

HAVE YOU BEEN BITTEN?

A thick blanket of fog snakes through the valleys of America. It hovers over the cities like a great depression. It blocks out light and brings an ennui that numbs the world it touches. In the blanket's shadows, the dead drag their feet, soulless and without the capacity to hope. They move through their life in drudgery, moving as little as possible—just enough to eat and to buy their drug of choice. Not feeling is not enough; they must shut off all echoes of life's call. They shut down and escape the lives they are living by drinking, shooting up, smoking crack, or smoking marijuana. To quell the voices that say, "You are not dead enough or numb enough to do it all again tomorrow," they escape. Those who still have some life in them try to function on pain killers, antidepressants or television. Still, somewhere deep inside of them, is the knowledge that there is something more.

Some of our young are under the illusion that they are alive, and they are frantic with misspent energy. They run every day, go to the gym, go to work, and check their social media 1000 times a day to see if they are important or relevant or "liked." Everything they do is projected outward to answer the question, "What do people think of me?" They are dancing as fast as they can on the edge of the sword of desperation. They have made themselves mirrors of their society and culture, only projecting what they think people want them to do, be, or feel. They are on a treadmill, following the hive as proof of life. There is no indication that they are any more hopeful as reflectors of life, than those escaping life.

Both of the scenarios above are symptoms of the toxic venom that has permeated our culture. The infatuation, draw, and addiction to Zombie movies, television series, and art are evidence that our youth are obsessed with the dead. The shows "The Walking Dead," "Z Nation," and "The Zombie Apocalypse," to name just a few of the hundreds of movies and television shows that portray dead people walking the earth, are bombarding our young with images. Why is this generation so obsessed? Do not blame the movies or the media; art is a reflection of life, and it portrays the symptoms of our cultural illness. Art and media are expressions. This generation has watched their parents check out and numb out. The "yuppie" generation decided that life was about getting up, getting the paycheck and then pushing the alarm silencer to do it again and again and again with no hope that life will get better. The boredom, the zoning out, and the self-medication of Generation X all began with the parents of the 1970s.

This is not a new virus. This is a virulent strain that has smoldered and crept out of the homes of the disillusioned, disenfranchised, disconnected generation of the Vietnam era. That generation once believed they could count! They could make a difference! They are the ones who started garbage recycling, Greenpeace, and who marched on campuses and in the streets to bring an end to the Vietnam War. They protested the war, greed, corruption, and wanton spending. They preached love, peace, and justice. They tried to save the whales, the trees, and those on death row. But they learned, one by one, that one person did not make a difference in the tide of pollution and hatred and greed. They tried to make a difference, but then children, jobs, life happened, and the boredom of day-to-day life took hold. They became shell-shocked, burned out by the sheer masses of needy causes, lack of resources, or cooperation.

The children of the Vietnam era, the present-day generation, know that something is wrong. They know, and they are obsessed with reflecting the sheer violence and death of this ennui. They are burned out from seeing all the violence on TV, but they want to identify with something in life. They either identify with the zombies or with the people battling for life. They either want to be the ones in control of death and dying, or they want to be the ones who put an end to the destroyers and the destruction. Maybe they identify with both, which overwhelms them, so they retreat to hide. Some might draw hope from characters that make it through and survive to fight another day.

When did all of this begin? Dating back to the beginning of recorded history, there are accounts of the dead coming back to life to battle the living. Most accounts occurred after a plague or a war from which dead bodies accumulated in a community. Then, eyewitnesses wrote or recorded what they had seen or what they envisioned. Some accounts are pure myth, some are ghost stories and bad dreams, and some are legends.

Historians say that the obsession with death and the fear of horrible ways to die begin with an epic catastrophe, like the plague. People who died from the plague were piled in common graves with hideous sores and dissolving body parts, which were openly visible to passersby. Some cities sent their dead down the river on barges to remove them, and the next villages were infected by these bloated Petri dishes of the plague. Nightmares must have permeated the societies affected. Stories of these bodies walking away or going into villages to destroy them were rampant. Stories of "boogie men" and distorted creatures emerged as well.

Rabbi Dr. Louis Jacobs (1920-2006) wrote in My Jewish Learning: "A golem is a creature made out of clay into which life has been injected by magical means. The Hebrew word golem means something incomplete or unfinished, as in the verse referring to the human embryo: "Thine eyes did see mine unfinished substance (glom)." (Psalms 139:16 KJV) While the notion that it is possible to bring to life an artificial semi-human figure is found in the Talmud, the term golem for such a creature was not used until centuries later. In Ethics of the Fathers (5.7), the golem is contrasted with the wise man and thus denotes a stupid person, like 'dummy' in English slang.

In a Talmudic passage (Sanhedrin 65b) it is stated that the Babylonian teacher Rava (fourth century CE) created a man and sent him to Rabbi Zera who tried to converse with him but when he saw that the man could not speak, he said, 'You belong to that crew (of the magicians), go back to dust.' The passage continues that the two third-century Palestinian teachers Rabbi Haninah and Rabbi Oshea, with the aid of the Sefer Yetzirah (Book of Creation), created a calf every eve of the Sabbath which they ate on the Sabbath. This passage implies that the Rabbis brought these creatures into being by white magic. It was later spelled out that in white magic, divine names, the creative powers in the universe, were utilized.

In the year 1808, Jakob Grimm, of fairy-tale fame, wrote: "After saying certain prayers and observing certain fast days, the Polish Jews make the figure of a man from clay or mud, and when they pronounce the divine name over him, he must come to life. He cannot speak, but he understands fairly well what is said or commanded. They call him Golem and use him as a servant to do all sorts of housework." This kind of legend evidently enjoyed a wide circulation. (1)

In the *Book of the Dead*, there are accounts of the same elements from the myth that appear in the Pyramid Texts, which recur in funerary texts written in later times, such as the Coffin Texts from the Middle Kingdom. The Egyptian accounts in 1550 BCE preceded the Golem of Prague tale but postdate the Talmudic accounts. The Egyptian accounts are of Osiris raising the dead as a hoard of soldiers to fight for him against Set. Later in the coffin texts of the middle kingdom (c. 2055–1650 BCE) and the Book of the Dead from the Middle Kingdom (c. 1550–1070 BCE) are more accounts of the dead rising. Most of these writings were available to the general populace, so unlike the Pyramid Texts, they link Osiris with all deceased souls. In the myth, he is able to raise an army from the dead to fight his battles using spells.(2)

In historical times, there were several battles and many plagues. These happened during that same period of time as the stories about the dead rising with missing skin and body parts. Fear permeated the minds of the masses. The walking dead are not the only monsters from these dark ages, wars, and plagues. Monsters that devoured and crushed societies, monsters that sucked the blood of their victims (Vampires), and shapeshifters who stole, robbed, and destroyed are depicted in every civilization. Unexplained horrors are attributed to these soulless entities. When things go awry in a nation, society, or culture, people seek the cause of the horror in the dark mist of their fears. Our nation, America, is attracted to these stories. Why now? How do we battle a vague infection of the hearts and minds? The visual media have reflected our fears and our obsessions with death and dying, in the forms of the zombie, vampire, and other American horror stories.

I have interviewed members of this target audience, and they have indicated that they are addicted to the stories because of the survivors. They want to know how to survive an apocalyptic event. They wanted to learn what actions they could take if the dead rise. In fact, they said that the bitten are just the infected. I suggested that they are attracted to these stories because they identify with them. This generation of 18 to 30-year-olds are involved in battles every day. They experience desperation, loss of hope, loss of identity, loss of respect, and loss of belief in the systems, culture, and government in which they find themselves living. They do not feel that they are making a difference in this world. When many of them graduated from school, they found that there were no jobs, there was a housing crisis, and their parents had lost their jobs, homes, and savings accounts in several of the economic and Wall Street downturns. They were witnessing this downward spiral without much promise. Some of them were in fourth grade when 9/11 occurred. They saw falling bodies and people jumping from buildings. They saw the fear and the horror on the faces of those around them.

In the aftermath of 9/11, they saw their families trying to cope in any way they could. Some were valiant in their efforts to get, or keep their jobs and homes. Many people were despondent and took to self-medicating as their situations became more distressing. Our children saw how we responded to crisis and loss. They saw us turning to Valium, OxyContin, Xanax, and Ambien to sleep and to caffeine to wake. As they saw us struggling to cope, mental health disorders began to steadily increase.

Zombies are a metaphor for our culture. They are reflections of how we are feeling and what we are fighting. We are both the Zombie and the Survivor. We struggle between the dark and the light and between life and death. Remember, most of the parents of these 18 to 30-year-olds lived during the Vietnam era—they had already had their fair share of disillusionment prior to 9/11. Now, they have lost their pensions, jobs, and homes, which they depended on to create their identities. These were the things that the "Greatest Generation" worked for after World War II, and their children had adopted their attitudes, beliefs, and morals. They pursued excellence within the status quo because they had come to understand that the rebellion during the 60s had not turned out as they had hoped. They became "Yuppies." They embodied the statement, "If you can't beat them, join them."

Have you been bitten? If so what now? Is there an antivenom for this plague? Is there a pathway to the light and to a more passionate life? I know that there is because I have experienced and overcome drama and trauma. It begins with changing negative beliefs about yourself, expanding your consciousness, and finding out who you really are. This search includes finding out where you fit into your culture and society and what you personally have to offer to make the world around you a better place. The personal identities found by this generation will lead to finding our National Identity once again.

My personal favorite of all Zombie movies is "Shaun of the Dead" (written by Simon Pegg and Edgar Wright). Granted, it is probably the least frightening of horror stories because it is pure comedy and farce. What I love about it is that the writers and producers offered the cure. Shaun, who is a teenage Zombie, sees a "live" girl, and something happens to him. He becomes interested in her. His interest in "something" begins a change in him. He sees her in color. Before, everything was in gray and white. But he sees her in color! After a short time, he sees the color of her hair, her eyes, and her clothes. As he makes contact with her, he finds that she is not repulsed by him; she is kind and sweet. As Shaun falls in love with this *live* girl, he begins to feel more emotions. He comes back to life. Love has set him free.

Obviously, this is a simplistic cure, but poetic license is a given in art and movies. There is something to this truth that love makes us more alive. What *has* truly been missing in all the social media available, all the selfies, profiles, and connections, is a true love of self. Everything is a mirror of what people want. Put your best foot forward! Only post inspiring comments! Show how great you are, or don't post. We are aghast at people who post hate and socially incorrect or politically incorrect statements, and we can only "like." If we don't "like," we don't post. Then, we are shocked when a friend commits suicide or overdoses. No one saw it coming. We are becoming more isolated by our devices than in any time in history. There is no one "checking in" on people personally. It is all texts, posts, and instant messages. Our eye-to-eye connection, our communication between the windows of our souls, has disappeared. We are losing what we love, and that makes us all weaker. There is a way out. Follow me...follow the sign posts, follow the stars—the path leads to your health, wellness, strength, and more of YOU. We all need that.

Chapter 2

AWAKE TO A PASSIONATE LIFE!

First, wake from your long sleep. Look around for the evidence you collected to prove to yourself that you do not count. What habits did you develop to stay numb to your life? What strategies are in place that keep you stuck in the drudgery that you consciously tried to avoid? What pains are in your heart and your body that became so intolerable? Who has been in your life that has hurt you, betrayed you, or angered you? Do you have energy vampires in your life—people who drain your energy? Do you engage in circular thinking or ponder dilemmas that also rob you of energy? Have there been key decisions you refused to make but instead you did everything possible to forget, evade, or push away? It is time to unburden the beast, clear the path, and slowly, but decidedly, climb out of the quicksand.

First, take a real assessment of where you are and what life looks like now. Write down all of the feelings you experience as you actually take a look at your life. Write down all the habits which have gotten in the way of what you want. Did you give up on yourself? Do you overeat or drink every night? Does spending money on yourself make you feel better for a moment? What do you do to fix your problems, that actually creates more problems? Maybe it is porn or hours of prime-time television that helps you escape. Most people use several of these strategies or even all of them. There is an epidemic of escapisms. No one is immune from using these strategies from time to time. How many times have you heard, "I was so tired-I just wanted to put my feet up and have a glass of wine and zone out." Or lately, it is "smoke a bowl and zone out."

Maybe you have developed one of this century's medical problems. Millions of people are being diagnosed with attention deficit disorder, clinical depression, sleep disorder, anxiety disorder, restless leg syndrome, and autoimmune diseases. Maybe you have been prescribed medicine that you have leaned on and that you have learned to depend on, so you think you do not qualify as or fit into the description of the "bitten." Maybe you think you have more "legitimate" reasons to medicate. Write down the reasons you need to escape. What about your life is so difficult that you need a vacation from it every night? Where did you lose your dreams and yourself? What are YOUR symptoms of this zombie plague? How deadly is your life? How are YOU self-medicating? All of these questions are tantamount in pinching yourself to see if you're real and shaking your head to wake up. Scream, "Wake up!" You have been in a modern, horrible nightmare.

NOW, are you shaking off the cobwebs? Where do you find hope? Hope can be fragile, and it can gain strength in three ways: managing your thoughts, managing your social networks, and managing your actions. There is one thread that will be a lifeline through the difficult task ahead. Faith. Some of you may not know much about faith, and some have a belief system that helps them with faith. In the Bible, it says, "Now faith is the substance of things hoped for" (Hebrews 11:1 KJ21) This means that if you have faith, you have the very ingredients you need for what you are hoping for. How do you build faith? The Bible also says that "faith comes by hearing and hearing by the Word of God" (Romans 10:17 KJ21). So, in the Word is the seed that sprouts faith.

What if you are not a Christian? You do not have to believe in gravity for gravity to work on you. Rain falls on the believer and the nonbeliever. There are principles which apply to everyone. Christians simply received instructions—they have a manual for an exemplary life. Still, many of them are even deeper in the fog. Believing is not a panacea for the virus; however, activating your faith is the cure. If you flat out reject these tenets, then discover what you do believe. Discover what you *do* have faith in. Some say themselves; others say a higher authority, ancient teachers, the ocean, the earth, or the universe. Gather it all; you will need to have as much faith in as many things, people, and ideas as you can to be able to beat the fog that is rolling over this land.

Neuroscience (another thing to believe in) is proving what the Bible said all along. Neuroscience is showing us that your brain can be trained to produce hope. So, you can produce faith by hearing other people's stories of surviving impossible situations. If you can't walk, you can listen to stories of people who were told they would never walk again but they got up and did it anyway through struggles and perseverance. Mirror neurons were discovered in August of 1990 by scientists studying monkey's brains. Several books about what this discovery means to psychology have been published, but one which I enjoyed is "The Empathic Brain" by Christian Keysers.(7) The discovery of mirror neurons makes us realize that we are not mere individuals but we see ourselves as a deeply interconnected social mind (7). The discovery has led to several experiments and has been likened to the discovery of DNA. It is far-reaching in its implications. What it boils down to is this: What we record in our vision activates these mirror neurons to make us identify with who and what we are seeing and act on the information.

You will need to protect yourself from unintended learning. The first step is to guard what your eyes see and ears hear because the mirror neurons will activate physical reactions. If you see someone pick up and eat an M&M, you taste it! If you see people dragging through their days asleep, you will begin to act like a sleepwalker. By watching videos or reading stories about people's victories over darkness, the mirror neurons in your brain will activate. They tell your brain to match or mirror what you see in the videos or books, in your behavior. Your mirror neurons will start to develop a new belief: "I can!" These new studies have proven what we already knew. Children learn by observing. We learn to walk by watching walkers. A person pole vaults at 12 feet, and then the observers believe that 12 feet are very doable. What we "SEE" moves us to feel, to sense, to taste, and to be empathetic.

It appears that in addition to visualization, thoughts and perceptions are just as important. Dr. Caroline Leaf has proven the old saying that "thoughts are things." She has written a book called "21 Day Detox for the Brain" in which she provides instructions to actually help the brain develop healthy thoughts. She is a neuroscientist who has explored the neuroplasticity of the brain. This refers to the ability of the brain to change (8). Her extraordinary videos show how the brain reacts to toxic thoughts. She reveals how the thoughts have actually caused neurotoxins to drip from the neurons during a toxic thought. These toxins make people physically sick. Dr. Leaf also shows what happens to the brain when it replaces the toxic thought with an "I can" message or positive or visually beautiful thoughts. These thoughts- lead to health. A negative way of thinking leads to death, and a positive way of thinking leads to life. I particularly like her example of a neuron branch that turns sticky and gray and looks like a dead tree. Then, she contrasts that image with the image of a neuron as it responds to beautiful thoughts, which looks like a green, leafy tree. These neuron branches shoot arches of light that resemble the Aurora Borealis.

Okay, I believe you have activated your mirror neurons, and you are beginning to believe that you "can wake to a passionate life." You are beginning to believe that you can do things that you did not even want to do. You are beginning to believe you can do things which had stopped giving you any joy or happiness. You are beginning to believe you can enjoy events, foods, and activities that had lost their color. You are like "Shaun in Shaun of the Dead"(6); color is coming back into your life. But, can your new hope go away? It went away before. How do you guard against a relapse into apathy? How do you exit the zombie nation for good? You must rewind your story to pre-bite. You must find out what life was like before you walked into the delusional fog that robbed your life of joy.

What did your life look like at its best? Did you once have a passionate life? When did you stop singing, dancing, laughing, and dreaming? What was life like when you did enjoy everything? What did it sound like, taste like, feel like, and look like? If you cannot remember, then observe people who seem to be very excited about life. Search for inspirational stories about people who nearly died or people who woke from a coma and then accomplished extraordinary things. There are resources for you out there. People's lives can be roadmaps for you to follow, much like a trail out of the mountains. Focus on these stories of victories and reawakening. Go to the bookstore and search for biographies of people who were lost or were beyond hope. Gather evidence of fabulous lives. As you record these stories in your brain, you will have built yourself a resource library for any moment you feel you are slipping away. These are resources for a wounded world: laughter, dancing, singing, and dreaming. To begin to want to do these things, you must observe people and mimic them.

Dance when you feel like sitting; sing when you feel like hiding; laugh when you feel like crying, and dream a new dream when you feel like life is difficult, and you want to escape. Fight all old negative behaviors and reactions to life events. Challenge yourself to do the opposite, and watch yourself begin to change. Research has proven that we can change our psychology by changing our physiology. By pretending to be happy, we become happier. By smiling or remembering someone who was laughing hard while telling a joke, our chemistry begins to align with these actions. The old adage "fake it till you make it" has been proven in biology. Our actions can change our beliefs about ourselves. Acting happy makes us believe we are happier. There are several neuropsychologists and cognitive behavioral therapists who use dance to heal the minds and bodies of trauma patients, Alzheimer's victims, and brain injury patients.

The article, *10 Ways Dance Strengthens the Brain* by Ruth

Bucznsky, Ph.D. (9) presents a list of benefits of dance for the above-mentioned conditions. To paraphrase her article, dance instills confidence, mental activity, connects the mind and body, breaks isolation, invokes imagery with movement, focuses eyes and ears as touch tools, increases awareness of the body within space, tells a story, sparks creativity, and increases rhythm and joy. In another article, *Dancing Makes You Smarter* by Jeremy Long, he argued that dancing results in increasing serotonin, which is a neurotransmitter responsible for several brain functions (6). The Bible contains several passages about dancing. In 2 Samuel 6:16 (KJ21) David is "leaping and dancing before the Lord." Psalm 149:3 (KJ21) encourages the use of dancing to worship God: "Let them praise his name with dancing!" Likewise, Psalm 150:4 (KJ21) urges us to "praise him with tambourine and dancing," just like Miriam.

After learning about neuroscience, mirror neurons, resource libraries, and behavioral belief stories, are you beginning to believe in more, more life, more joy, more laughter, more fun, and more value for your life? A part of you may be worried that it is much too risky to put yourself out there. It is easy to dream about more in life and even easy to see it in your mind's eye, but to act on what you see and what you choose to believe may seem overwhelming. It is safe to want more out of life, but be assured the herd will not want you to escape.

CHAPTER 3

THE BATTLE FOR YOUR SOUL

There is a battle for your soul! There is a battlefield beyond the veil, a spiritual warfare fought by principalities, and it is happening NOW! You will have to know who you are and what you want if you are to win back lost territories of your soul. Who are you? In the previous chapters, we have been examining what you do to escape and why you need to escape. We discussed self-medicating. Most of you have a feeling that you are different, but you are unsure about how you are unique. Many of you felt as though you did not belong in your family, your school, your neighborhood, your community, or even your culture. Your separateness screamed so loud that you scared yourself. It was easier to reflect everyone and everything around you so that the pain of being lonely could be avoided. You became mirrors of family, friends, parents, and teachers. You hid your true self to become more of what was considered normal and acceptable. Being different or fighting for yourself was too high a price to pay; however, a higher price is now being paid because you are so far away from your true identity that the retreat may seem impossible.

What are you battling for? You need to reclaim the territory of your soul. Losing your identity to reflect everyone else's light has dimmed your own light. This is the biggest battle of your life. Does this seem overly dramatic? The numbness you have been existing in has fogged your thinking. You could continue to drudge through life as a member of the dead, the zombie nation, but you are reading this book, so that is now almost impossible. You have been given just the smallest dose of anti-venom: hope. Decide each day, maybe each moment, that you are worth fighting for. You were born to be the dream that you had as a child. Where is that dream? Where did you put it? How do you find yourself, or how do you even determine where the battlefield is? I ask again: Who are you really? Knowing that will help you know what you are fighting for and how to fight for your soul. You matter! Trust the fact that you matter as an act of faith! Let's begin with finding a part of yourself which we can create into a mighty defender of your soul.

This discussion must begin with an understanding of archetypes, which have been used for hundreds of years. The usage of the term has been expanded by comparative anthropology and the Jungian archetypal theory. It was further expanded and modeled for use by Tony Robbins and Cloe Mandanes founders of RMT.com (RobbinsMandanesTraining) with fellow co-founders Mark and Magali Peysha, whose body of work involves *Strategic Intervention*. The work of Michael Bennett of Bennett Stellar University -as well as talented life coaches and psychologists- has furthered the use of and the understanding of *archetypes*. The most interesting concept in these works is using parts of yourself to embody one of these archetypes, or characters, which are used in integration therapies.

Indigenous people often used headdresses and masks to

help a person embody the animal they most wanted to emulate. Totems were used in Native American cultures to create a source of power and protection over their village. In some of these cultures children would be given the name of an animal. The belief was that the characteristics of that animal would be added to the child's spirit and be reflected in their character.

Other approaches have been to assign powerful titles, such as poet, warrior, princess, king, queen, magician, lover, diplomat, sage, or monk. I like to use elements of the earth: stars, oceans, trees, mountains, and rivers. These descriptions are limited only by imagination. They can be used to receive information from your deepest subconscious knowing. If you ask any of the archetypes a question, you will find the wisdom and the information seem perfectly fitted to their type. The wisdom comes from you, but dividing yourself into characteristics and characters allows you to probe each for more information, which is similar to mining them for data.

Pick your defender now. Let us create the details of this part of you. If you were a superhero, who would you be? Superman? Wonder Woman? Would you be a mythological character? What special powers would you have? If you were a princess, warrior, or a king, who battles the enemy with your generals? What would you be like, act like, and feel like? Choose something now! What does your Super Self look like? What is he or she wearing? What weapons are carried? How do those weapons work? Create as much detail as needed. What other characteristics does this defender of your soul have? Is it wise, kind, gentle, disciplined, strong, muscular, fast, tall, or tiny? Is it diplomatic, aggressive, wary, or strategic? Where do they stand in relation to your physical body?

Where could you put it? Could it walk through walls, fly, disappear, or shoot lasers out its eyes or hands?

Now, reassess the way your defender looks, dresses, acts, reacts, and feels. Breathe as much life into this picture as you can. When you get a clear picture, touch your heart, wrist, or somewhere on your body that you can use to anchor this image. Each time you think of this Super Self, touch that spot and feel the life of that part of you. The more detail you provide and the more frequently you utilize this image and anchoring process, the easier it will be and the quicker you will be able to see and empower that part of yourself. When you have done these dozens of times, you will only have to touch that anchor to activate your Super Self.

Okay, you have your defender. Do you have a sword and a shield? Is it safe to come out? Let's find the core of you. Let's find the soul you have hidden from everyone. Trekking down to the core of your being can be arduous, but you have left clues. You have left bread crumbs to your secret self. Some believe this is a spiritual silver chord that has always been attached to you but ignored. Returning to your earliest memories is a good way to begin. You can return to when you first dreamed of a life for yourself, when you played and laughed, and when you were a child. Remember the days when you were first discovering what you liked to do, eat, hear, and feel. Remember the first games you played with others. Remember the first time you found out that something was not yours! Remember when you first wanted something. Feel the passion and the rage you felt having to share or "be nice." The lessons were necessary, but running away from your SELF-has not been the answer. It is time to gather what was lost and collect all of the crumbs.

You can begin by discovering what you value. You have probably heard the term "core values." When psychologists, sociologists, and the media adopted this term, it became popular but possibly misunderstood. To some, the term refers to a number of beliefs that form the core of a value system. To others, beliefs, morals, and mores lie at the very core of self, which make up core values. I use a combination of *Neuro-linguistic* Programing by Richard Bandler, (12) and *Strategic Intervention* techniques (Mark and Magali Peysha's work) (11), Milton Erickson's methods, and my Bennett Stellar University training to help you assemble these beliefs. These scholars are masters of all the techniques which I have mentioned, and they have developed their own body of knowledge. It is important for you to leave behind the beliefs which have not served you. Instead, focus on what you believe is at the very core of what you find important, true, and of greatest intrinsic value to your life, culture, country, and relationships. Maybe you think it all boils down to one word. Some have said everything of value reduces to its greatest common denominator: love. Some say *honesty* or even *cooperation*. Ask yourself key questions: What do I value? What is most important to me? What is integral to a good life? Whatever the answers are, they make YOU stronger.

Next, gather what you love, such as people, places, things, events, songs, instrumental pieces, cultural music pieces, plays, TV series, movies, books, authors, inventors, comedians, politicians, philosophers, and theories. Then, add core values or beliefs that make up the body of what you find important to a valuable life. Take time with these. Write out each thing that made you smile, gave you joy, or made your heart hope. Start a notebook, and keep a page about each of these topics. Leave enough space to include pictures, photographs, magazine articles, or anything you might want to include as you go. For example, you might have several pages for the people you love so that you can include a photo next to the name. For music or culture, you might want to include visual media as well or articles or sheet music. For TV series, write down the main characters and the storyline.

Someday, you will want to remember more. Treat the entries as though you are writing them for someone who does not know you to give this person an idea of who you are based on your entries. Don't just catalog your likes or interests; detail them. Make sure that you can add to all of these pages whenever you like. You may have to conduct research to find out what sparks your interest if you have traveled very far from yourself. Some people use pictures from magazines of the most basic things they enjoy, including catsup, butter, lemon pepper, lipstick, eyeliner, makeup, shoes, dresses, suits, hats, coats, pancakes, or French toast. Do you prefer butterflies over dragonflies? Pine trees or oak? Try to capture every detail of what you like, what makes you happy, or what you love. All of these things make you stronger because they help you learn who YOU are!!!

Now that you know what you value and what you like and love, you can combine all of this to create something you can give to your Super Self. One of my clients mixed it all into a drink that gave her Super Self a strong sense of right and wrong and made her invincible against the gray fog of apathy. One client compressed it into a diamond and put it into the solar plexus of the Super Self. The Super Self was able to direct light towards the diamond, creating a laser-like focus and an ability to cut through the most difficult or dense problems. One client made a cloak of armor out of all that she loved and valued. You will discover what you need to do. You could need a suit of armor or a sword and shield to protect and defend you against those who want to diminish who you are and what you are here to do. Once your defender has been effectively envisioned then you will be prepared for battle.

There is a battle for your soul! There is a battle to steal your light and control what you believe and what you do. There is a battle for your brain and a battle for your personality. The media wages war on your psyche by proving to you that you are not good enough the way you are. (Ephesians 6:12 KJ21) "For we wrestle not against flesh and blood, but against principalities, against powers, against the rulers of the darkness of this world, against spiritual wickedness in high places." Cultural pressure says that you must buy this product or that, fit into this size or that, or believe this or that. Billions of dollars are spent controlling the masses, and they tell you they are helping you be an individual while they entice you to buy the cookie cutter mold. Developing critical thinking or questioning is discouraged all the way through school, college, and the business world. Conforming to the nine-to-five work life or consumer-oriented society began in your crib, and unless you are prepared to go to battle, it will end at the grave. Don't drink the Kool-Aid. WAKE UP!

You will have to prepare yourself to step onto the battlefield for your heart, mind, and soul. Your soul should command your brain. Your brain has not been designed to be what it has become: a reactionary organ. It is designed to be a command center for the soul to control the body by controlling the brain. When you decide that it is time to take your life, your energies, and your amazing purpose back, when you decide that there must be more to life than the fog you have been living in, when you are ready to say enough is enough, then you are ready to activate your powers and to learn how to LIVE again! It is not for the faint of heart! Prepare your body! Gather your armor and your weapons of war!

"Therefore, take unto you the whole armor of God, that ye may be able to withstand in the evil day and, having done all, to stand. Stand therefore, having your loins girded about with truth, and having on the breastplate of righteousness, and your feet shod with the preparation of the Gospel of peace. Above all, take the shield of faith, wherewith ye shall be able to quench all the fiery darts of the wicked. And take the helmet of salvation and the sword of the Spirit, which is the Word of God, praying always with all prayer and supplication in the Spirit and watching thereunto with all perseverance and supplication for all saints" (Ephesians 6:13-28 KJ21) NOW step into your Super Self and call your angels! Begin your training on brain control and thought management!

CHAPTER 4

BLOOD, BONE, HEART, AND BRAIN

Does it seem like you have no control over this blood, bone, heart, and brain of yours? Do you think you are a victim of an environment, culture, or big pharmaceuticals? It is time to take control! Step into your "super-self." You have the power to take back this vessel! The blood, bones, heart, and brain of your body are only a house for the soul, the spirit, and the consciousness that make up your personality. There is a kingdom that was designed for you! It is time for you to climb into the control tower and take over the controls. The spirit breathes divine purpose into your soul. Your soul was designed to control the brain, and the brain controls your body. It is time to decide to take over the brain, to begin managing memories, thoughts, and beliefs. You will need to challenge your thoughts *before* they become things. You will have to depose the evil dictator who has had control over everything that has been happening in your life. Then, begin to cleanse your blood, regrow your bones, and heal the heart. This will all be accomplished by your brain using neuro-technology to create new neuropathways.

Once you have completed the neural detox, you will need to rebuild and reassign your conscious guards. Their new job is to reintegrate systems to create cooperation for a new consciousness that aligns with your soul's purpose and with the divine spirit living in you. Your final step is to sit on the throne of your kingdom and take your crown. Your kingdom has come. Did you notice how many times the word "will" was used? You were given a free will, and God won't go against your will. You must exercise your "will." Jesus said, "The Kingdom of Heaven is like a mustard seed" (Luke 13:19 KJ21), and "come take your inheritance, the kingdom I prepared for you since the creation of the world" (Matthew 25:34 KJ21) because "the kingdom of God is within you" (Luke 17:21 KJ21). Take your kingdom!!

How do you take over the brain? Remember, I said, " The brain controls the systems and manages the memory and your thoughts." But, it really does so much more. It catalogs everything you think, hear, see, say, and touch into bits of information. It organizes beliefs and theories around its perceptions of this information. If left unmanned, it becomes a reactionary tool. Without direction, it will make assumptions based on the data it receives. As we know, with any mainframe or computer, whatever you put into it is what you get out: "garbage in, garbage out." Audio and visual information combined with *stored* information are all the brain has to go on, and then it creates a reaction-formation pattern. Left truly unattended, it reacts the way the movies, songs, media, news, politicians, teachers, parents, and any other influential or important events have programmed it to respond.

But, what would you think or feel if all the data you were

allowed to receive was directed by your higher self, the spirit-filled divine entity that came to this body with a purpose for life? How would everything change if you created your own software to record, edit, and sort data according to "whatever is noble, whatever is right, whatever is pure, whatever is lovely, whatever is admirable—if anything is excellent or praiseworthy, think about such things" (Philippians 4:8 KJ21)?

You might be asking yourself how you could live in this world and only think about those things. You might be saying, "I would have to close my ears and my eyes to stop the barrage of violence, chaos, destruction, heartbreak, and tragedy that happens around me every day." But, the directions given in the Bible are terrific editing tools for your brain. It is a framework with which you decide what you will "think upon" and what you will reject or sort out for the trash bin. Just like every computer has a trash bin for things not worth keeping, you can have a button for discarding worthless thoughts or beliefs. Eliminate all beliefs which do not serve your core values. Discard all image sources that rob you of peace, joy, and hope.

Tragic memories must be sorted, and they require a decision from you to answer, "What do I do with this?" It is an excellent question. If it is in your power to turn the directives of Phil 4:8 into an action, then direct the body to take action. "Love" is an action word. Love is a verb. Taking clothes or food to someone who just lost their home is an appropriate action for tragic imagery. If the event is too far away or overwhelmingly difficult to act on, then your best action is to direct it to the King. Your protocol for all things not manageable by the body is to kick it upstairs. Your divinely inspired Soul will take it to the Author and the Finisher of our destinies, the King of all Universes. You have a kingdom; He has authority over all kingdoms. Your soul has a direct line to tech support of all types. You can call for divine help!

Deposing the evil dictator of your brain reminds me of the movie "*A Space Odyssey*" when the computer, "Hal," decided he has learned enough to be in control. He decided that he had gathered the information and that he knew what was best for the crew and the ship. He planned his takeover, then slowly and methodically implemented his plan. Your brain has been left relatively undirected and has taken things in its own processing direction. Just like Hal hacked all the programs of the ships computer, your software has been hacked! You are the software.

In the previous paragraphs, I discussed the need to control your thoughts. You will need to decide what you think that your core values are, then reprogram your brain with that in mind. Before you do that, you will have to get rid of all of the old programming. Imagine that you have to climb the control tower to throw the insane controller out. Imagine saying, "Sorry, I will take over from here. You can stand down." Imagine taking the knobs, switches, and computer keys over and reprogramming your brain for great blood pressure, blood sugar, digestion, clean arteries, a healthy liver and kidneys, and well-lubricated joints. What does your body need? Do you need to reset the calorie burn, the cholesterol levels, or the cartilage and collagen in the joints? What do you need your new program to mend? Maybe you need a DNA overhaul.

Expect a barrage of resistant thoughts and events which

will pull you towards old patterns of responses. Be vigilant about these slings and arrows. Events can occur that you might immediately respond to in a reactionary way. Hold every thought to your core values, to your deepest truths. If you react in an old, unproductive pattern, forgive yourself quickly, and then process the information using your new framework.

How do you clean your blood, grow new bones, and heal your heart? Your soul now controls the brain. It is imperative that you spend time being mindful. What is broken in you? What medical or spiritual problems have you been experiencing? Dr. Carolyn Leaf's book, *"Twenty-one day Detox for the Brain"* (8) is a very good place to start. She suggests that you replace old thoughts like "all my relatives have high blood pressure and they all have passed away by 65" with this message: "I am healthy, and my blood pressure is 110 over 70." She recommends that you say positive outcome messages for seven minutes a day for 93 days—three cycles of 21 days—and then witness the miracle that your brain has performed on your body!(8)

Replacing negative thoughts and beliefs is very important. The universe hates a void. Rejecting negative thoughts is not enough. That is why it is so important to decide what you want. Decide that you can have what you say, then decide to say it. Ask your doctor to tell you the normal parameters for all markers in your blood. What are normal liver enzymes, blood sugar, cholesterol, and blood pressure levels? See it, meditate on it, hear yourself say you have it, and choose to believe you have it. When you meditate, remember the more detail you create to control the outcomes, the more you will change the neuro-pathways. The more emotion you say it with, the more your brain will believe it.

We have found that the younger the client is and the extent of the quantity and quality of the events that they witnessed, heard, or felt determine how deeply ingrained the event becomes in their subconscious drivers. For instance, hearing that your family has always been bad at math has a higher impact on your subconscious at five than if you heard it at 50. The younger you were when the negative message was implanted, the more it impacts your life. Gathering all unintentional learning that formed into erroneous beliefs and then purging them is a great start!

You have guards that determine who and what has access to your consciousness. These guards keep information that you have gathered over your lifetime which is not of value from reaching your belief system. You can thank them for being keepers of the knowledge, but let them know new information is available now, and you prefer it over the old messages. Tell them that you have deemed the old knowledge to be unreliable based on science and education or experience. You can give them new assignments, ones which serve you better! Any part of you not in agreement with that, can be reeducated and reassigned to be of greater value.

Some old patterns may have served you, kept you safe, and organized your world in a manageable way as a five-year-old, but they are totally restrictive and almost ridiculous for your adult self. Fears and phobias develop instantaneously, but they are completely illogical to the adult self. You may say to yourself that you have no control over your tremendous fear of spiders or heights, for instance. The truth is-your computer brain received a powerful, shocking message that you are not safe and programmed a flight or fight response in you that was an overreaction to the stimulus. Fears and phobias are the easiest to neuro-linguistically program out. Reframing and re-experiencing the event in a more resourceful way can remove the data error and create a new way to experience fears. Once you reassign your guards, integrate the parts of yourself which were not cooperative with your soul's purpose, then you are ready to take the throne of your life (8).

The soul's throne of your kingdom is to be occupied by your super-self, the monarch. All thoughts, actions, dreams, data, and goals are to be determined and judged as valuable or useful only by the King. These determinations will be made based on your core values, your truths, your divine purpose, and your passions. Only actions or beliefs in full alignment with your purpose will be allowed into the kingdom. Your life and the expressions of your purpose will reflect only those truths and those values. If you have beliefs that do not serve you, examine them again; challenge them all, based on your true core. Everything "will" be aligned under the umbrella of the kingdom, under the protection of the kingdom, under the laws judged to be right by you, the ruler.

What does your kingdom look like? Who are your helpers, what is your influence, and what treaties do you have? Who are the palace guards? What is your power? Your kingdom has come: "the kingdom of heaven is within you" (Luke 17:21 KJ21). It is up to you to assign parts of yourself to perform specific tasks. You may have to review all your contracts, covenants, and treaties. You may have to rebuild your policies to protect your sovereignty. Taking the throne of your kingdom is a daily event. It is an intentional process to prove to the kingdom that authority still belongs to the monarch. Rise every morning ready to exercise your authority and to reveal today's orders. Show your entire entity who is in control!

CHAPTER 5

CALLING ALL ANGELS

When you were a zombie, when you were sleepwalking in the valley of boredom, you could not see or feel the power around you. You were unaware of your abilities and strengths; like Sleeping Beauty, you awaited the kiss. The kiss was the anti-venom for the poisonous prick of the finger. Remember that the hero, Prince Philip, came to wake her with love and hope. He was compelled to respond to her beauty. He knew a kiss would wake the princess. The anti-venom for the poisonous needle was delivered by his kiss—an outside force. Nothing *she* did woke her. It required someone bringing her the medicine of a kiss. LOVE!

This book is brought to you by angels which I have sent to awaken you. Maybe you think this is farfetched, but think about how you got this book or how it came into your mind or hands. It is my intention and my faith, just like Prince Philip, that my love and hope will awaken you to your life. How did I know I could send you angels? Through the power of prayer, a receptive and eager heart to help, and a revelation of your need. Your stories came to me: "Wake up O sleeper, Rise from the dead, and Christ will shine on you" (Ephesians 5:14 KJ21).

I was praying about how to activate my guardian angels. During my prayer, I was given a vision. I saw dozens of angels on the rooftops, porches, steps, and yards of my neighbors. Some houses had two; some had ten. They looked bored, pruning their feathers. Some were asleep or just still. I asked, "What is this, Lord?" The Lord said to me (not in an audible voice but in my heart), "They are unemployed angels." I asked, "How can they be unemployed? Didn't you send them?" He replied, "Yes, but once assigned to you, they are limited by your free will. They will guard and protect you, but they can do so much more. They can do anything you ask them to do that fits within my laws. You can order your angels or assign them tasks. They want to help…they are waiting for instructions." That was quite a revelation to me, and seeing all those unemployed angels made me weep. I was shocked when I realized we all had this tremendous power to impact our own lives, and more especially the lives around us, but we had fallen asleep to our divine natures and our true destinies.

So, let's take an inventory of who angels are and what they can do. The best resource for this is the Bible, which says more about angels and their operations than any book in history. They are described as supernatural beings created by God before mankind. They are agents or messengers. The descriptions and biblical references are provided below.

They are:

- Created—Ps 148.2 and Col 1:16
- Spiritual beings—Heb 1:13-14
- Immortal —Luke 20:36

- Holy — Matt 25:31
- Innumerable—Heb 12:22
- Wise—2Sam 14:17
- Powerful—Ps 103:20
- Elect— 1Timothy 5:21
- Meek and Respectful — Jude 8:9
- Sexless —Matt 22:30
- Invisible—Num 22:22
- Obedient— Ps 103:20
- Possess human emotions—Luke 15:10
- Incarnate in human form —Gen 18:24
- Organized in ranks and orders—Isa 6:24

(The full scriptures are included in the back of this book under this chapter's heading.)

They have been given assignments to guide, protect, deliver, gather, direct activities, comfort, and minister to those they are assigned. They are known to be musicians and singers and to herald the message of the Lord. They have been known to slay, fight, defend, and perform any assignment they were given.

There were some angels who fell from heaven and mated with humans, and their offspring were known as Nephilim. They are recorded in Genesis 6:4 (NIV) "The Nephilim were on earth in those days and also afterword when the sons of God went to the daughters of humans and had children by them. They were the heroes of old, men of renown." They known to be giants in the land. Aside from fallen angels let us assume that you have been assigned angels of Light from heaven. Let us assume you have at least one. I have seen that many people begin with two. I began with two, and now I have been assigned many more—a legion of six thousand angels. Sometimes I feel I have far too many awaiting assignments, and sometimes I feel that I do not have enough. I must admit that keeping six thousand angels on assignment is difficult, and I am in the training stages. I am learning to delegate to warrior angels to do battle and physical work, and to comforting angels to give comfort, protect, and send messages of hope and love. This book is a result of awakening to the power of angels around me.

How do you wake your angels up? The first step is to imagine them with you. The second is to give them a task. You can "think" the task. For example, you can ask them to go ahead of you to protect you from injury, to bring a piece of information to you that you need, or to find out what is needed to complete a project that you are working on and bring the resources to you. Whatever you could ask a soldier, employee, or partner, you can request of angels. You can give them spiritual tasks or material tasks. You can ask them to bring to you ideas, wisdom, or even to purify the land around you. You can ask them to stand vigil or to take your love to someone in need of comfort.

In this case, since you are just now experiencing angels, you might want to learn as much as you can about how they work, who they are, and what kind of power they have. In the Bible, angels have been described as messengers from God. So, they can receive and send messages! One angel killed every firstborn child in Egypt the night of the first Passover of the Jews. One angel killed a whole encampment (2Kings 19:35 NIV): "that very night the Lord's messenger went out and killed 185,000 men."

Jesus told Peter, "Do you think that I cannot call on my Father and he will at once put at my disposal more than twelve legions of Angels?" (Matthew 26:53 KJ21). As you can see, even one angel is more powerful than any modern army.

Your next step in managing your angels is to become aware, every day, of the power and the help that has been gifted to you by heaven. Beyond the veil, beyond the guardian angels in the Heavenly Realms, is *Help*, longing to be given to you. Activating your faith, activating your imagination, inviting dreams, and asking for more wisdom and more evidence is a great beginning. Faith is the substance or (evidence) of things hoped for (Hebrews 11:1 NIV)! So, you must activate your faith that you have angels before activating your angels. You must gather the evidence that they are obedient by keeping a log of your instructions and the results.

If you are not a Christian and you do not feel that the Bible is a source for you, then you can read first-hand experiences in books and stories that other people have written. You can borrow their beliefs or faith until you have established your own, but know that there are also fallen angels who will try to appear as angels of light and misdirect you. You must guide yours according to your core values and remember that gravity works for us all. We do not have to believe in gravity. For those of you who do not want to explore the Bible as a source, there are many books on angels on Amazon.com that are somewhat secular, but almost all are spiritual by nature.

You will soon begin to think, "I have angels. Now, what do I do?" Learn to use your angels in their traditional roles. Send them to comfort a friend, loved one, or even someone you saw on the news. Ask them to inspire you with messages of hope and grace each day. Ask them to bring new light and life to you. Ask them to awaken you *to* the beauty that is each new morning. Have them remind you of your value and purpose. Ask them to bring back all your happy memories. Ask them to gather the moments that you laughed and to help you recall all the faces involved in every joyful moment that you have experienced. Ask them to bring you new friends, new mentors, new teachers, and new masters in your field of study. Ask them to nudge you in the direction of opportunities. Ask them to minister to the people you love each day and to remind you to be grateful.

After I was shown unemployed angels and was given so many to direct, I began to think about the biggest problems in my neighborhood. What could I have them do? Where could they do the most good with the immediate problems? The biggest problem that we were having was that the lake (Liberty Lake), where I live, was drying up from far too many days over 100 degrees. It had become so warm that the lake dried and turned over, it looked like a three-inch oil slick mixed with mud. The milfoil liked the heat and was overgrowing at the bottom of the lakeshore. The county decided that the problem was so bad that the milfoil would need to be poisoned. The result was toxic algae. Signs were posted not to swim or let animals into the water. I left angels in charge of a bucket brigade to heaven: taking dirty water up and bringing clean water down. I left for a cruise through Greece, Rome, and Turkey for 17 days. When I returned, the sign was down, and I was able to see the bottom of the lake from the dock. I had not been able to see the bottom of the lake at the end of the dock for years! The next task

I gave them was to fill the lake with fresh water. We had rainfall for about 18 days straight.

Now it is winter, and we have had more precipitation in the past month than we had all of the last year. Some of you may believe this is just the weather and a coincidence. Many cultures believe that prayer changes the weather. Because they believed, they gathered evidence. You might think because I believed, I gathered evidence and I tested my command. If you think this then you are right! You will see as you send, as you ask, and as you command, that you will acquire plenty of evidence that they are completing your tasks.

Okay! You are still reading! I have not lost you yet! It is time for you to practice envisioning your Delta force. There is more beyond the veil than your guardian angels; you have a heavenly host wanting to help you. My favorite prayer for all of you is: "I pray also that the eyes of your heart may be enlightened in order that you may know the hope to which He has called you, the riches of His glorious inheritance in the saints, and His incomparably great power for us who believe. That power is like the working of mighty strength which He exerted in Christ when He raised Him from the dead and seated Him at his right hand in the heavenly realms, far above all rule and authority and power and dominion, and every title that can be given, not only in the present age but also in the one to come" (Ephesians 1:18-20).

Even with heavenly help, you will need armor, so I pray this for you all as well: (Ephesians 6:11-13, NLT) "Put on the full armor of God so that you will be able to stand firm against the schemes of the devil. For our struggle is not against flesh and blood, but against the rulers, against the powers, against the world forces of this darkness, against the spiritual forces of wickedness in the heavenly realms . Therefore, take up the full armor of God, so that you will be able to resist in the evil day, and having done everything, to stand firm."

You are going to need help for this battle that you cannot see. You have angels to command to help you: "Are not all angels ministering spirits sent to serve those who will inherit Salvation?" (Hebrews 1:14 NIV). Have faith that they are yours to command. Believe that you can use them according to the word of God. Using that word and using your will to fight the battles, enlist your angels to do the things that angels were designed to do!

Gather your Delta force, equip yourself for the battle, and take your territory. Command your angels to do the things which need to be done to expand your influence, your ministry, your gifts, your abilities, your light, and your knowledge, and receive their ministry to you. What is the territory you want? What resources do you need to acquire that territory? What and who are you battling? Have faith: "That night the angel of the Lord went out and put to death a hundred and eighty-five thousand men in the Assyrian Camp. When people got up the next morning, there were all the dead bodies!" (2 Kings 19:35 NIV).

Your job is less difficult if it is totally within the will of God to expand your territory. In His Word, Jabez cried out, "Oh, that you would bless me and enlarge my territory! Let your hand be with me and keep me from harm so that I will be free from pain! God granted him his request." (Chronicles 4:10). So, you are fully within the word and the will of God to ask your angels to help you. But, remember who the source of those angels is-not you!

They are not powerful in and of themselves. All authority has been given to you to access and order your angels, but you must know who the ultimate authority is: the Creator! Praise opens the heavens. You have your Delta force to add to all of your resources: "for He will command his angels concerning you, to guard you in all your ways; they will lift you up in their hands so that you will not strike your foot against a stone" (Psalm 91:11-12 KJ21).

I keep a journal of Angel stories about how, where and when angels have shown up to protect, serve, comfort, gather, and investigate for me. Keep your own journal of instructions and a history of completed tasks, and you will KNOW that angels are working for you, with you, ahead of you, behind you, and beside you. Remember, "You have not because you ask not" (James 4:2 KJ21). ASK.

Chapter 6

TREKKING TO THE NEW JERUSALEM

Your New Jerusalem is calling you! I will assume you are doing everything that has been covered in the previous chapters. You have been preparing to take your territory. You have learned how to call back all of the pieces of your soul—to strengthen yourself with all that you love. You have taken control of your brain, using your core values to run your program that decides what information is of value or is true. You have decided what you will believe. You have gathered your tools and resources. You have called your angels to defend and guard you on your journey. Continue your inventory for your travels.

NOW, you have to start where you are. Are you ready? Have you packed all of the tools and resources into an easily accessible box, cart, or backpack? Look around you to make sure that you have all you need. Re-assess each change that you have made. Be honest about those changes. See all the things that you will not be taking with you. Make a conscious decision about the people who will be with you and those you will need to eliminate from your life.

Some people will want to stay in zombie land and will

fight you for leaving or changing. Some people were never with you but only fed on you. It will be difficult to keep your resolve. You do not need to be combative or even direct. You can just stop answering their calls and stop engaging in activities with them. You can and should be kind as you decline invitations. Alcoholics do not continue to hang out with alcoholics, once they admit they have a problem and begin treatment.

Maybe the person who has helped to lock the chains that bound you to your enslaved, barely alive self was your spouse or a family member. It seems impossible to leave because of children, financial entanglements, or your religious beliefs. This is a difficult problem which needs super faith to navigate through the obstacles. Retreating within the confines of your own strengths and values, before demanding more from life, will be your best, first move. Start being true to your newly rediscovered strengths and values. You may have to separate until you are stronger. However, many can start changing themselves by exploring all that makes them strong right where they are. Gather all your resources, within and without. Change you; *you* are the only person you can change.

You will have to quarantine yourself by surrounding yourself with only people who have been given the anti-venom. Your best friends are awaiting you, and they will applaud your passionate life. You must start where you are, but you also must not stay there. If you are living with people who are struggling with addiction, it can be much more difficult for you. You will need to gather even more resources to leave Egypt.

Where are you going? Do you know? What does that passionate life look like? You will need to send out your angels to gather intel about your Promised Land. They will guide you, and the light inside you will lead you to information from people, the web, bookstores, and television. Yes! Television. 'When the student is ready, the teacher appears.' When I began writing this book, no one to my knowledge in the Christian world was even talking about angels. Then, led by the Holy Spirit, an awakening occurred. I have heard no fewer than three pastors talking about Angels!

So, believe me, you will find resources and sources for intel that you never thought about. If you decided your passion and purpose is to be a baker, you will suddenly have ideas, see books, learn tricks, and receive inspiration in the most unusual places. This will be true no matter what your passion or purpose. This phase really involves gathering information about what more you will need to do, find or acquire to expand your territory both internally and externally. You are ready to go because now YOU MUST LEAVE EGYPT!

In Egypt, the Jews suffered for hundreds of years in exile and in slavery. They were held in bondage, starving, and completely at the mercy of the Egyptians, who wanted to control them and use them for everything they needed. When they left Egypt, they had nothing of their own to carry. Nevertheless, they carried out the precious gems, silver, and gold of their owners and enslavers. After the plagues and the Passover, the Jews were told by Moses to ask their owners for all of their valuables. Unbelievably, they were given jewels, precious stones, gold, silver, and the most valuable items in their enslavers' households.

Much of what they were given, the jewels, gems and precious metals, was used to build the first temple. What is more, not one person died in the desert! When they left, they spent 40 years in the desert before they were allowed to go into the Promised Land. The reason for the long delay was faulty intel and careless actions. Several of their scouts decided that the Promised Land was too difficult to take. They said there were giants in the land. If they had believed what they had been promised, they would have arrived there long before. Why did they not believe? They had been provided for so well on the way. Not even a strap on a sandal broke during their time in the desert. The Lord provided water from a rock, and wafers of honey called manna for food. They were protected and provided for, and yet they feared!

They had a personal walk with Yawe, and yet they still wanted to play it safe. They grumbled about having to eat honey wafers. So, they were swarmed by pigeons. They ate those and became sick. They are an example to us all that it is a matter of trusting God. They are an example that tells us that you have everything that you need to take the Promised Land. So, what is your Egypt like? Are you ready to leave your enslavers, your naysayers, and your own disbelief to obtain your Promised Land of milk and honey?

Your Egypt will not be easy to leave. You have become comfortable in your ennui and fog state, even in painful slavery to your surroundings. Expect to be chased down by your enslavers. They may call after you and make you remember what you were or what they expect you to be. You will have to keep your eyes on the future while you are running. Do not look back at the dead—they are still zombies and do not understand that you want to escape what you know. Because of the work of faith, which you have already accomplished, you are heading into the desert with everything you need.

Camels are desert animals, but they are metaphors as well. A camel carries all it needs to survive inside itself. It carries the water it needs for days. They hold the excess water in the lining of their stomachs, and they store food in their humps. This allows them to go long periods without food or water. Their source of continued life, through dry and hot days, is inside them. This is you. You have now built your strength; you have water that makes you never thirst.

Faith is the substance of things hoped for. ALL that you need to get to the Promised Land is in you. Especially now, you will need to manage your fears. There are ways to do this. In your mind and heart, create a place that is familiar to you. A place of peace, comfort, beauty, and joy. It can look and feel like a special day in the mountains when you felt so connected to the source of all life. Or it can be a magical place of metaphorical beauty like the world of Avatar. It can be a beach you visited where you felt the warmth of the sun on your skin and the sand on your back and between your toes. It can be that place where you hear the water lapping at the edge of the bay. Fill in all the details of your place of peace. In this place, feel an immense source of love. Feel yourself being loved and enjoyed, and feel the love you experience for the place and spirit you now have with you.

One person described being held by his father in a warm pool. The father was teaching him to relax, to float on his back. He trusted his father's hands were still there as he floated on the water. Even though he could not physically feel the hands on his small back anymore, he knew his dad was there just beneath the water's surface, waiting to catch and protect him.

Once you fill in all the details of being in this safe and beautiful place, squeeze your right wrist with your left hand. This is called anchoring. You anchor this vision and experience inside your body. Practice envisioning this beautiful place and your anchoring technique seven minutes a day for a month. Whenever you are afraid or experience doubt or anxiety, you can squeeze your wrist and immediately go to your special place. It will calm your body and rest your mind. The more you practice, the better the tool is for managing your thoughts and your fears. These relaxation techniques are taught by Milton Erickson, the father of hypnosis,(13) and many other types of teachers, such as yoga teachers, Neuro-Linguistic Programers (NLP), and strategic interventionists (11).

Where is your Promised Land? What is your New Jerusalem? What does it mean to you to have a place waiting for you? What does it mean to have a place of provision (milk and honey), a place of peace, and a place of hope and new life? What does it mean to have a place to build your dreams and live out your purpose? What is the light and what is the passion that was put into you? You have now learned that whenever you become afraid of the future, you have a tool to access your inner peace and comfort by using imagery and anchoring.

You create a new visual *promise* the same way. First, listen to your soul. Your soul knows why you were sent to earth. It knows why you have been called to this time and this place. It knows what special gifts and talents you have been given to share with the world. It knows what you will need to accomplish your mission. Your soul knows your promise and what you have been promised. Listen to your soul, and begin to write the vision of your passion down. Here is an example. A singer may imagine themselves using their music as therapy for the lonely and the disenfranchised. Their Promised Land is a life of creating this music and sharing it. They may envision where they will wake each morning, knowing they will impact lives. They may envision recordings or stages or even event halls. They may envision a home, a family, and children. They might see themselves living a life of purpose and passion.

You may have a completely different dream you wish to accomplish. But, you get the drift. The dream was put into you. A friend told me this: "Break down the word desire. DE means from or of and Sire refers to The Father. Hence desire literally means from the Father." Build your DESIRE. If you don't know what it is, ask: "Reveal the concealed." Ask God "show me a dream bigger than I could ever ask for or that I could ever imagine for myself" Commit to dreaming about it every night. Remember Jabez asking the Lord to expand his territory.

Those of you who have gathered resources- your angels and all the things that make you strong- are ready to have even more faith. How do you obtain more faith? By increasing your knowledge and your resources and by asking for divine help to develop and expand the vision, your faith will grow. Whatever you see, conceive, and activate in your mirror, neurons can replicate in the material world. You will walk it out in faith using all of you: your brain, personality, soul, the divine spirit, and all of the helpers beyond the veil. What dream was put into *you* as a child? To fly? To sing? To own a business? To invent?

How will this gift, talent, or dream look when you get to your Promised Land? What aspects of yourself will be awakened? How will you use all of the gifts you were given? What are your gifts? Write it all out, and then see it grow. See it as a territory, as your influence, as the details of your dream. Then, expand it; make it bigger. Imagine blowing into it as if it were a balloon. What needs to change for it to be bigger? For example, if I were encouraging a singer to have a bigger dream, I would have them imagine their success, their audiences, their Road Warrior touring bus, their guitar or piano, their crew, their performance wardrobe, and the home they return to- as well as the love they put into it all. After imagining it, I would ask them to develop the details of each part of their dream. Determine what else is needed then bring it up a notch such as copywriting their process, producing signed guitars, sellable wearables, branding every part of their life, and building their estate vision.

It may seem like an impossible journey, but every journey of a thousand miles begins with one step. People with one leg, no legs, no money, or no transportation have made thousand mile journeys, impossible recoveries, and complete life transformations. Your journey to your New Jerusalem will start the same way: with your right foot or your left. Get up from your seat right now! Even with this book in your hand. Take one step, and say with resolve, "I am on my way! I am on my way to my Promised Land. I believe I will be guided. I believe that everything I need has been put inside me and around me to accomplish my divine purpose! Nothing will stop me. I may have been delayed, but I will not be denied." Then, step into the Red Sea *with* faith that the waters WILL part.

Chapter 7

ALIGNING WITH THE STARS

It is time to align with the stars. Leaving Egypt does not mean you are truly free from the memory of it. Yes, it was horrible, but it was the devil you knew. You left, and you were excited and hopeful; inevitably you will enter a dry spell where you might yearn to go back to what you knew. During this dry spell, all the excitement and direction you had developed may seemingly disappear. Do not think for a minute that you will be any different than the Israelites, who grumbled in the desert because they were tired of honey biscuits and living in tents. You will have your own desert experience.

One thing I know for sure is-when you are in the desert, the stars are the brightest because there are no competing light sources. They are so brilliant and beautiful! It is time to lay back and watch the starry night pass by. These stars are another metaphor for you; probe them like a dream. What do they mean? It might be time for you to think about the really bright stars in the field, or occupation in which you want to shine. This is the time to really dream about where you are going and what you will do. What do you want to become extraordinary at, and what do you want to be? You have read the chapter about finding out who you are and what you love. You have been working on visualizing what your territory would look like. It is time to lay back and go back in time and space to see how far you have come and what has been driving you.

As you are lying there watching the night sky, metaphorically ask yourself some questions which will help excavate your gifts. What gifts do you have? Where and when were the gifts planted in you? Is it a gift of the spirit, a gift of the flesh, or a gift of the mind that you received? What dream did you have as a child? Do you remember getting excited about something that you saw, heard, or felt? What inspired you to learn about a subject? Which subjects did you like even though they were difficult? What dream was whispered in your ear? You might have been numb so long you can't remember, or maybe it is just on the tip of your memory. What one thing did you do better than others that surprised you? Did you ever say, or did anyone ever say to you, "Oh, you are so good at that!" Write down the subjects and events that you remember. I am sure by now you are beginning to receive several revelations about your interests that ignite some passion. If none of this has sparked a memory, think now of things you *know* you can do well and things you have pride in being able to do.

There is a purpose placed inside of your DNA. You were designed with a passionate purpose in mind. I recently heard that we are all 99 percent the same DNA, and the 1 percent different cells are on the tongue, fingertips, and eyes. You are uniquely designed to be you—you process all information differently. This is extremely interesting just on a spiritual level. Your tastes and your speech have power over your brain. Your fingertips not only identify you, they also help you navigate all you experience. Your eyes are considered the windows to your soul. Now, that is interesting on several levels. What this discovery suggests is-what you see, say, and feel are how you acquired your personality. Your one percent difference is where you will find your individual gifts and your divine purpose.

The Bible says that the purpose of human life is to praise God. There are many ways to praise the Creator. Offering yourself and your resources back to your community may be the finest praise. Using all the ways you are different, I believe, is what we all need. We all need you to be what you were designed to be. You have a purpose! NOW is the time to become passionate about it. Ask your angels to breathe on your fire, your passion. Ask God to reveal the concealed in you. Ask for dreams to come at night that will ignite a new passion in you. Write about the things you love, the things you hope for, and the things that make you feel alive. Now it is time to learn more about yourself.

When you were remembering back to your childhood, did you see anyone who encouraged or believed in you? Who did you admire? Who was kind to you? Who spoke words of hope and life over you? What were the things that made you feel seen, heard, and understood? Who did you want to grow up to be like? These questions will begin to open the branches of memory and help you recall more of the light which has been hidden in you.

You may have had a teacher, neighbor, or family member who really believed in you. Everyone has had at least three people who have had a positive impact on their lives, even if it was only momentary. There is so much inside you. There are so many people who were just like you when you lived as a zombie. Some of the people who believed in you, still do. These people recognized light, hope, and genius in you. Sit in the dark, and quiet your mind. Shhhhh. Listen! Hear your song calling you like a siren. Your soul is just vibrations and frequencies. It has your song and is longing to play it for you. Listen. It will ignite your fire.

Your next step on this journey is to find out who the stars in your field are. Look up, and look around. Who does what you have dreamed of doing? You may have competing gifts. Congratulations! This is a wonderful problem to have. How and where can you use all of you, and what would that be like? Find these stars in your field, locally, in your state, and in your country, then study, investigate, and research how they became experts in their craft. If you can find someone local, call and request an internship or even an interview to find out more. It takes ten thousand hours to become excellent at your craft. That is a lot of hours! The good news is that they will be hours doing something you LOVE. Not like getting up every day and facing only drudgery and boredom. It will be hard work, but then it is said that if you love what you do, you will never work a day in your life. Now that is the greatest retirement of all! You may have to work to get to that place of doing what you love. You are well on your way just knowing what it will take to begin. Choose the constellation in which you will play.

It is time to begin your internship. Once you have found out who is excellent at your unique gift, then it is time to practice all of the techniques they use to be a star. What did they do to get where they are? Break down all the steps because, unless you are so extraordinary that you woke up one day and were equipped to accomplish your dream, like child prodigies, there are no substitutions or shortcuts for doing the work. Write out each step they took, and find out who they know. Write down who you know. What pieces are missing in your grand puzzle and dream? Do you need equipment, education, tools, space, or a plan? Whatever is missing to reach the stars, find and use it. If you need education, get started now! During your education, spend lots of time observing and recording what you will need once you arrive at your New Jerusalem.

For example: if your dream was to be a great defense attorney and you just now are starting your long period of education, then during this time, take five minutes a day to write out what you will need the minute you get your law degree. Line up your final year's internship now. Start calling the law firms you may be interested in joining when you are done. Speak with your fellow law students who may have the same dream, and then work together for a while. Find the greatest, strongest, and most ethical defense attorneys where you want to live and work, and then keep requesting interviews with them. What habits do they have? How did they gather their resources? Who do they know? If you cannot find great examples, expand your search to include people who are the best in other fields. Follow their work ethic, their organizational skills, and their actions. Study people who have excelled and let them model exactly what to do to be the highest and brightest of all stars. What will you do differently, and how will you distinguish and identify yourself in your constellation? Name your Star!

Chapter 8

BREATH OF LIFE

When you were a particle in the plans of God—just a spark of light that broke off during the Big Bang—God knew who you were and who you would be. He carved your name into the palm of his hand. He has been awaiting you. He has been waiting for you to come to the Source of all life. It has been painful for Him to see so many of His children bogged down by lies, difficult and wrong choices, and the spell of a lost world. He has been hunting you down and sending you help, direction, and God-incidences to help you see that He loves you beyond measure, even if you don't know, don't believe, and don't think there is life after NOW. Gravity and other principles that He designed for this universe work for believers and nonbelievers alike. The sun that warms your face on a cold day also warms life on earth and it does so for all humans, not just those who believe in the sun's warmth.

The plan that is in your DNA was not alive until you breathed your first breath. The breath was your soul given to you the moment you gasped. (The first breath that you took when you left your mothers womb.) Everything was activated by that breath. But, life is a process. When you were an infant, you were totally dependent on others to care for you. Now, you are old enough to begin to care for yourself. The most important thing that you can do is to breathe. I know it seems like a given because it is an autonomic response. Everything in us demands oxygen, but there are many things that hinder breathing. We have to become conscious of our breath. The Lord says he is the Breath of Life. You will need to learn to control your breathing and provide that divine fuel source to your fire. OXYGEN blown onto an open wound accelerates healing; blown into your gift, it will ignite a raging fire. It is imperative to learn breathing techniques to learn how to control your breathing and use it to gather your power and force of life. Progress is a process. Keep breathing. Everything on the physical plane has its impact on the spiritual plane.

When you can't breathe because you are afraid, sick, tired, or in terrible pain, you need mouth to mouth to keep your lungs open and working until you can breathe on your own again. Get help, ask for help, reach out to your divine HELP. Be aware of the things that make you stop breathing or that change your breathing pattern. When people are in shock, pain, or anxiety, they will tense their entire body against the pain, like they are pushing back. When you notice yourself doing that, take three deep, cleansing breaths. Make sure you are breathing out twice as long as you are breathing in, or you can hyperventilate. Keep the breaths slow and even. Learn to do meditation-style breathing as well. This will make you mindful of one of the three cornerstones of life, which are air, water, and food. Without oxygen, you are dead in three to four minutes, or at least your control center/brain is dead. Each time you "lose your breath" or have your "breath taken away" by something, immediately *decide* to breathe. Say, "I choose to breathe through the pain and the fear of what I am experiencing right now." Keep breathing!

Be aware-words fly on a breath. One of the most important words in the English language is "inspire." To inspire literally means "to breathe into." Inspiration then is being breathed into by someone that brought oxygen to your plan, purpose, or being. When God breathed into Adam, He gave him life and purpose. In the language of our culture, it has much to do with what we see, which activates our mirror neurons to believe we can do something. To control the adverse effects of our culture, we must decide what we want to mimic or model. We are inspired by our mirror neurons to mimic what we see. We believe it possible to do great things by seeing others do great things. We may be inspired by things that no one else understands or perceives because of our unique DNA.

Therefore, we are inspired internally and from the divine to create new music, science, inventions, and narratives. We are genetically wired with these neurons so that as babies, we would see walking and thus emulate walking. We would hear and see people talking, and we would emulate speech. We would see people jumping, riding, running, and pole vaulting, and we would realize that whatever we see, we can do. "Whatever the mind of man can conceive and believe, it can achieve." Napoleon Hill "<u>Think and Grow Rich</u>." Some would just call that positive thinking, but now science has proven that we are fundamentally wired this way. If you want or need the inspiration to achieve your dreams, you will want to find inspirational stories to feed the fire, the desire, and the will to emulate. Watch! Hear! Do!

Understanding all you can about breathing will help you

to learn to feed your spirit. Breathing life into your goals is a matter of feeding them inspiration each day. Being mindful of breathing, gathering inspiring stories, and consciously breathing them into your spirit will give you hope and energy to move forward. Small actions towards your intended outcomes will give you proof that you are definitely on your way to your Promised Land. You will see the growth, see your improvements, and see the goal becoming closer.

Take time to enjoy your successes no matter how small. Time spent looking around you and enjoying the scenery right where you are, will give you all kinds of clues that you have left Egypt, and you have taken control. Continue to be mindful of breathing into the space that you are in. If you are drawing in a breath from God then you will be breathing that into the space you are in. Acknowledge what you love about where you are now, what you have learned, who you have met, and who has helped you. Then, breathe these thoughts into your picture with gratitude. Be grateful to your angels, and give them the task of reminding you to breathe and to move.

The world was breathed into being! The author of this world spoke it into place: "In the beginning was the word, and the word was with God and the word was God" (John 1:1 KJV). Claim your position as a child of God. One excellent way to discover the power of your breath is to speak your world into being. Take a supernatural breath, like the one given to Adam. God breathed into his form and gave Adam life. Take a deep breath from the heavens, and state what you want. Learn to speak the blessings and the dreams over your life while modeling the perfect ONE.

The Jewish sect that produced the Virgin Mary was called the Essenes. They have a practice of using the words in the Bible formed as an "I am" message. Using this concept- say "I am blessed, I am loved, I am strong, I am a divine gift giver, I am the righteousness of God, and I am Light in the world." Then use your desired goal as I am statements. I am an exquisite guitar player or singer or architect. Say it with passion and purpose over your life, and use your breathing to give it truth and life. You can speak all of your hopes and dreams in this way: "I am life, I am hope, I am a blessing, I am a joy, I am kind, I am mercy, I am grace, I am a mother, a father, a friend, a sister, a brother, a mentor, a lover, and a mover and shaker." Whatever you need to say over your life and the lives around you, say it!

Here are a few Bible Verses that can be spoken over your life as "I am" messages:

I am holy and without blame before Him in love (Ephesians 1:4 KJ21).

I am born of God and the evil one does not touch me (1 John 5:18 AMP).

I am complete in Him who is the head of all principality and power (Colossians 2:10 KJ21).

I am the light of the world (Matthew 5:14 KJ21). We are salt and light!

I am His elect, full of mercy, kindness, humility, and longsuffering (Colossians 3:12 KJ21).

I am called of God to be the voice of His praise (Psalm 66:8 NLT).

I am God's child for I am born again of the incorruptible seed of the Word of God which lives and abides forever (1Peter 1:23 KJV).

I am more than a conqueror through Him who loves me (Romans 8:37 KJV).

I am part of a chosen generation, a royal priesthood, a holy nation (1Peter 2:9 KJV).

I am a spirit being alive to God (Romans 6:11 KJV).

I am the temple of the Holy Spirit (1 Corinthians 6:19 KJV).

There are many ways to explore the value and depth of breath. You have been spoken into being, and you have been infilled with breath. One of the ways you have been infilled is the light that was put into you. When we want and ask for the divine to infill us, blow on our fire, and breathe with us our vision into the world, then we conspire; we breathe together with the divine. Conspiring and breathing together form a much stronger vision. When we learn to listen to that still, small voice in our soul, which knows our purpose and knows our gifts, then we are listening to divine guidance. In the Bible, this is called the Holy Spirit. Jesus said that he had to leave his disciples, so the Holy Spirit would come and dwell in them to guide them. Jesus said his disciples would do greater things than he did, meaning miracles, because of the power of the Holy Spirit in them. If you can believe this, if you can wrap your mind around the fact that Christians have the Holy Spirit in them, then you can see they are more powerful than they know. However, sleeping and sleepwalking, not being fully ALIVE, is just as prevalent in the Christian community as in the general population of zombies. Taking the leap of faith by saying, "I have a HOLY ONE living in me," will help you accept that there is help living in you. With the HOLY SPIRIT in you, guardian angels outside of you, and all of the help above you, the creator of heaven and earth, YAWE, you will have your new Life Force.

YAWE means the breath of Life and was the Hebrew name for God. It is not said but *breathed*. Ya in, and We out. Try it! Breathe "YA" in, and then say "Wey" as you let out your breath. Practice envisioning, breathing in the breath of God and letting it cleanse you and bring oxygen to the fire in you. Imagine you are an appliance, and you are plugged into your source of power. Conspiring and breathing with the living God will help you become all you can be and increase all the territories of your life and influence. When you were a zombie, you were barely breathing and were dragging aimlessly through life. Breathing the Divine will make you a bright flame that can be seen from very far away. Your life force will make you warrior strong! The miracles of healing and love will be yours to share with everyone around you.

Ezekiel 37:1-14, 21st Century King James Version (KJ21)

37 The hand of the Lord was upon me, and carried me out in the Spirit of the Lord and set me down in the midst of the valley which was full of bones,
2 and caused me to pass by them round about; and behold, there were very many in the open valley, and lo, they were very dry.
3 And He said unto me, "Son of man, can these bones live?" And I answered, "O Lord God, Thou knowest."
4 Again He said unto me, "Prophesy upon these bones and say unto them, 'O ye dry bones, hear the word of the Lord.

5 Thus saith the Lord God unto these bones: Behold, I will cause breath to enter into you, and ye shall live.
6 And I will lay sinews upon you, and will bring up flesh upon you, and cover you with skin, and put breath in you, and ye shall live; and ye shall know that I am the Lord.'"
7 So I prophesied as I was commanded; and as I prophesied, there was a noise, and behold, a shaking, and the bones came together, bone to his bone.
8 And when I beheld, lo, the sinews and the flesh came up upon them, and the skin covered them above; but there was no breath in them.
9 Then said He unto me, "Prophesy unto the wind. Prophesy, son of man, and say to the wind, 'Thus saith the Lord God: Come from the four winds, O breath, and breathe upon these slain, that they may live.'"
10 So I prophesied as He commanded me, and the breath came into them, and they lived and stood up upon their feet, an exceeding great army.
11 Then He said unto me, "Son of man, these bones are the whole house of Israel. Behold, they say, 'Our bones are dried and our hope is lost. We are cut off from our parts.'
12 Therefore prophesy and say unto them, 'Thus saith the Lord God: Behold, O My people, I will open your graves and cause you to come up out of your graves, and bring you into the land of Israel.
13 And ye shall know that I am the Lord when I have opened your graves, O My people, and brought you up out of your graves,
14 and shall put My Spirit in you and ye shall live, and I shall place you in your own land. Then shall ye know that I, the Lord, have spoken it and performed it, saith the Lord."

Let Him breathe into your dry bones then rise up to take *your own land!*

Chapter 9

THE WAY OF THE MASTER

You have left Egypt, decided who you want to be, found the light and gifts inside of you, and identified the stars in your field. You have learned to breathe into your body and into your vision of a passionate life. Your 'dry bones' have come ALIVE. Now it is time to intern with a master. Learning to walk in the shoes of a master is the next step in nourishing your genius and training your spirit to fill it's divine purpose. You may need to pick several field masters to train under or learn about, especially if you are blending your gifts to create a new platform. For example, a sound engineer will need to train in music, technology, and artistry. Techniques and proficiency in music and technology will not provide a new engineer with the edge needed to be a master. They will want to see and hear what passionate people in the field have been able to create. For instance, the first in that field, Phil Spector, created what was dubbed "the wall of sound"; however, his genius led him to drugs and murder. It is imperative, when you are looking for masters in the field, for you to understand that genius can drift quite close to insanity. Find people in the field who have kept their sanity and have developed their craft with integrity.

Once you have picked the men and women in your field

who you want to learn from or emulate, then begin to study them and their habits. In this phase, you do not have to limit yourself to one. Find as many masters in the desired field as you can, and study their lives and their work. Learn from their mistakes and their successes. This will shorten your process. People learn from their mistakes. You will make many of them, but you might as well learn about common pitfalls and follow the way of the true masters who are more creative due to their mistakes. The extent to which you are gifted in your desired field will only help if you have an equal drive and passion. How many people who were extremely talented gave up because it was not a challenge for them or because it was too easy? This happens frequently for athletes. Quite often, the best equipped or most gifted will not be the winner of the race.

I have heard many stories of talented people, such as someone who could sit down and play anything on a piano in childhood but does not play at all as an adult. Some of the most gifted singers in the world will never be heard or known. The best runners, the most talented athletes are rarely the winners. There is something about "genius" that can lead to less productivity. It is better if you have some talent and incredible drive. Those who want "it" the most will spend the time it will take to become the very best and brightest in the field. So, if you think or wonder if you are talented enough to make it, then know that hard work is the best tool for your path. Find the masters who are confident and humble. Read their histories and study their work. If they are alive, attempt to interview them. Make a list of questions that you would ask. See how they got where they are, and look at your own life to see if you can apply those techniques and methods of success to your path. There is no reason to blaze a new trail unless you know a better way. Make a list of everyone you are learning from and what you have learned. Record what you value about their work and the way they do the work.

Once you have found a master in your field, your internship should begin. You may not be able to have an official internship. Time and distance may prevent that, but you can begin to study what the master has done. Research everything you can find on what their work looks like. How did they do it, and who helped them accomplish their mastery? What are you missing? Do you have weak areas? Do you lack tools or resources? What things will you need to learn? Map the master's strengths and all of their weaknesses. Then, map out all of your strengths and your weaknesses. How will you set yourself apart? Do not focus on this too long because you have much to learn from them, and you will need to access your determination, inner drive, and your respect for them to research their life. Watching, learning, copying, practicing, and repeating are parts of becoming a master. Eric Clapton, arguably the best guitarist of our day, says it takes ten thousand hours to be a master at anything. Stay humble and teachable. It is important to be a sponge; later, you can squeeze out what you don't need and keep what you do need.

Once you have been able to replicate the techniques, the details, and the content of the master you have chosen to study, it is time to go deeper. If you have been able to intern directly, then this part will be easier in some ways and more difficult in other ways. Learning to breathe in the very nature of your mentor and making it part of your meditation practice will help you bring the master's inspiration into your work. What is the message of your master? What does his work try to say or communicate to the world? What is his passion or purpose? Ask more and better questions of your mentor. This is a technique of Jewish mystics, to ask better questions. If you are emulating a master who has passed or is far away or speaks a different language, then it may be a little more difficult to immerse yourself deep into the mindset of the master, but it can also be easier in some ways. Allowing yourself to probe your imagination and actually develop a storyline and a personality for the master you are studying, can be quite empowering as well as being a creative way to focus on their genius.

Practice visually stepping into the shoes of your mentor/master. As you live your day, as you imagine your master would, what is your day like? Who do you see? Who buys your work? Who do you influence while embodying their life? What are the choices and changes you encounter? How much work do you do? How often do you play, sleep, and exercise? How balanced is the life you are living? What things have you had to give up to be a master? How is your inner life? Are you conflicted about the sacrifices that you have made? What additional inspiration is necessary to take the next step? How do you remain inspired to do the work you do every day?

While you are walking a mile in their shoes, keep notes. How would you change the sacrifices for more balance? Be very honest. There may be moments in which you are disillusioned or even overwhelmed with doubt. It is imperative that you know that with great destiny comes great doubt. They are a married pair. Whenever you entertain doubt, erase it, and embody the destiny. Envision exactly the outcome you desire, live in it, and breathe into it. Spend time in an extreme and exaggerated moment of faith. Fear is **False Evidence Appearing Real.** (This acronym came from Dennis Waitley) Hebrews 11:1 "Now faith is the substance of things hoped for, the evidence of things not seen.") Each time doubts surface, CHOOSE FAITH.

About halfway through the ten-thousand-hour journey to mastery in your field, you and your work will have already been noticed. Be aware that now people are really watching you. They want to know if you are the real deal. They will want to see if you have the character to stick it out and to continue on your journey. Some may be hoping you quit. Conversely, they may be afraid you will leave them behind. You may have had to leave some of them behind already, and that will anger some and hurt others. Mend all the fences you can, but keep your integrity and your dream alive. Real friends will want you to succeed and will want to be a resource for you. Make sure you nurture those friendships because they will be part of your inner strength. They will get you through lonely and difficult moments.

You are well on your way, and people will want to follow you. Where you lead them is integral to your final story. Imagine yourself forty years from now. Imagine what you want to say about yourself, what others will say about you, what your angels will say about you, and what God will say. Your life is a message to the world. What is the message, and did you adhere to your core values as you achieved mastery? What kind of path did you leave behind, and who has followed in your footsteps? Did you help them along the way? In what ways have you given back to those who long to do what you have done? If you can put yourself in the shoes of the student, the teacher, the master, and the friend, then you will be able to access the grace and the kindness necessary to be happy in the end. Know that where you go, people will follow. If you have been mentored-mentor along your *Way*.

CHAPTER 10

THE LIGHT ON THE HILL, HADES, JUPITER, THE EARTH, AND THE MOON

"In the beginning, God created the heavens and the earth, now the earth was formless and empty, darkness was over the surface of the deep and the Spirit of God was hovering over the waters. And God said, 'Let there be light' and there was light" (Gen. 1-3 KJV). Later in Genesis, God puts stars in the sky and a "great light to govern the day and a lesser light to govern the night."(Gen. 1:16 KJV) In the first four chapters of the Bible, God gave us the sun, moon, and stars. Why? Light is necessary for trees that make oxygen for us to breathe, for food that we eat, and for the waters of the earth to provide for plant life. Light is a source of joy for us, and it serves as a muse for poetry, inspiration, and metaphors.

What kind of light are you? Are you like the light on the hill that feeds on its own source during the day so it will glow in the darkness? Before electricity, lamps had to be filled. People prepared the wicks and oil each evening so that they could burn. I was in Ephesus last September (2015), and I saw a mile of pillars that supported bowls of oil at the top of the columns. They lined the stairways and walkways of the city. They were a light in the darkness. These columns have remained for two thousand years, and they are a physical and spiritual manifestation of the importance of light to all of us. They are a great example that light will find a way, vessels that hold light will survive, and evidence of light will last forever.

Are you like that light on the hill or on dark stairways? Are you filled by day to glow at night? Do you have your own source of power? How do you replenish your fuel source? Is it continuous, like electricity, or refilled and used up, like an oil lamp? Are you so bright and powerful that you can bring ships safe into the harbor? Does your light attract wanderers and represent a beacon of hope, the way a lighthouse does? If your light shines this way all the time, you are rare. If not, maybe there was a moment where you were that hope, that directional light, attracting the lost to the safe harbor. It is possible that you aspire to be this kind of light. If so, you need to learn a lot about darkness. I know that I ask several questions, but it is to extract your story, to get you to ask yourselves these questions. The more that you know about "you," the brighter your light will glow.

Darkness is relative. Is the sun just over the horizon? Is there a moon? Is the last light of day still reflected on the night's clouds? Hades is the representation of darkness; it is a place where there is no light or life. You might have believed that Hell was an interchangeable word for Hades, but it is not. When I was inspired to use this chapter heading, I believed this as well. I have researched the things that the Lord outlined for me to include in this book. This chapter discusses some of the research.

The Old Testament teaches that there is life after death

and that people went to a place of conscious existence called Sheol. The wicked were there (Psalm 9:17; 31:17 NIV), and so were the righteous (Genesis 37:35 NIV); (Job 14:13 NIV); (Psalm 6:5 ; 16:10; 88:3 NIV); (Isaiah 38:10).

The New Testament equivalent of Sheol is Hades. Prior to Christ's resurrection, (Luke 16:19-31 NIV) describes Hades as being divided into two realms: a place of comfort, where Lazarus was, and a place of torment, where the rich man was. The word hell in verse 23 is not "Gehenna" (place of eternal torment) but "Hades" (place of the dead). Lazarus' place of comfort is elsewhere, called Paradise (Luke 23:43 NIV). Between these two districts of Hades is "a great gulf fixed" (Luke 16:26 NIV). It seems that Hades is a place of the dead. Those who are without life or light are lying in the "great gulf fixed" (4).

When you were a zombie, you moved as though you were alive, but you were just a skin bag of emptiness or darkness, like an expanse. There are those around you who are still "empty bags of darkness," but if you have read this far, you will have taken the anti-venom, that life-giving kiss. You have breathed oxygen into your soul by turning inward and finding your passion and purpose. You have been mentored, and each thing that you have learned has expanded your influence. You are not in Hades. You are alive. It is important to know that others are in a metaphorical Hades. You may have been there yourself, but you walked out. Look back only to see how far you have come.

The nature of light is that it has several variables. There are many ways to experience light and to be light. Some people, who seem very bright, very passionate, and exciting, who have great star power, are merely like Jupiter.

Jupiter has no mass. It is a gas ball. It is the largest planet in our solar system, yet it has no solid center. It is surrounded by bands of debris and particles that absorb and reflect the light of the sixty-six moons that orbit. It only reflects the dark and the light of what is around the planet. We see actors who dazzle us with their abilities to represent various stories or roles—both light and dark. When interviewed, they are often quite shy. They do not seem to have their own personality but rather reflect the personalities around them. They are whatever we want them to be, and they have no solid core inside. They are imitators of the people around them, and they magnify larger than life. Many people envy and worship these people.

Some "larger than life" people, who are worshiped by the masses and are in the news constantly, end up in rehab or therapy. They are empty planets. They want to be you! You are the real story and the true character—the one they want to portray to win an Oscar! YOU! That said, I do not believe all actors or fabulous singers are like Jupiter. I do believe at some point in their lives, they attempted to hide their emptiness by being large and loud. They became examples of the people everyone wanted them to be. If you are like Jupiter, if you have found it safer to be a reflection of light, then it is time to "be." You have found your core, your divine flame, your passion, and your purpose, so you can never be a Jupiter again, but you can play one. Never lose a skill.

Is your light sometimes like the blue planet Earth? The earth is a beautiful place to exist and to emulate. The water on the earth is like a mirror, and it shines blue into outer space. Earth does not have its own source of light but absorbs the light of the sun and enjoys the light of the moon. It has been given a special role in the heavens. If and when you are like Earth, consider this. You take in the light of the Source as you hold the ground and the water. Your absorption of light creates the perfect environment for all life to grow, survive, and thrive. You are a safe haven, and you provide a loving environment. You are attracted to these professions: doctors, nurses, gardeners, farmers, caregivers, mothers, and teachers. When you walk into a room, people immediately feel more grounded and centered. Their hearts beat slower, their shoulders drop, and their anxieties diminish. You have loving arms that receive. Most of us have been this to someone.

Most of us have "hats," or personas, we put on to emanate our light in a form that is comforting and appropriate in the situation. The important thing to remember is that we rotate into positions of light bearers and light receivers. We can metaphorically be any type of light we can see or imagine. Harness that thought!

What do you feel when you think of the moon? For me, I am surprised and delighted when I turn the corner on the road to my mountain home, then suddenly see the moon bright in the sky. I am in awe, and the sight inspires a feeling of magic in me. When I hear there will be an eclipse or a blood moon, I leave my house to find a vista. It is always a joy. It is a perfect representation of being a light in the darkness. The moon does not have its own light, but it does have a source for its light; that source is the sun. The moon is a large reflector of the sun. When the sun is on the other side of the earth, the moon shines into the night sky. On the lake in front of my house, the moon creates a light display of silvery diamonds. Every night and every season bring a new light, a new placement of the moon in the sky. When my children were younger, I would wake them in the middle of the night to take them out on the deck to see the full moon. It is not visible from our deck during some of the fall and winter months, which made it spectacular to view when we could.

Why does the moon inspire so much romance and self-reflection? If you are the earth, who are your moons? If you are the moon, what is your light source? If you are the moon, who receives your light and inspiration? When you shine into the darkness, where and what is that darkness? When you wax and wane, why? What makes you brighter, and what makes you a thumbnail in the sky? I may not be amazingly inspired by a thumbnail, but believe me, I am always grateful for even a sliver of light. It is a reminder that the heavens are watching. As a child, the Man in the Moon was a mystery that was visible and verifiable. My mother told us to remember that even in the dark, we are being watched. We were told that the light in the dark was a reminder that we were loved and being watched over. The metaphor illustrates that we are never totally in the dark.

Imagine that you can teleport yourself to any light or light source in the heavens. Stand in the great expanse of darkness—Hades. Imagine where you were and how you felt. As zombies, you were little more than dust and ashes barely in motion. Stand there. Now put your Superman suit on, hold out your arm and fist, and soar to Jupiter. Experience being empty, but be aware that there are shadows of light and dark around you. Imagine your sixty-six moons reflecting the sun's light. Imagine you are the largest anti-mass, gas ball in the sky. What does it feel like to have the attention and to be a reflection?

Now soar to the blue planet Earth. Be Earth. Feel what it is like to be a large vessel of water rotating in the universe. Feel the earth, and smell the forest; breathe the mountains in, and feel them rise out of your hope. Feel the growth and the life in the water and on the land. Every living thing grows and emanates out of your very being. Feel and see the people, animals, and plant life that are nurtured and restored by your very being. Feel yourself receiving the warming light of the sun and the dazzling light of the moon.

Now, stand on the face of the moon, and plant the flag of "You." Imagine being there and receiving the brilliance of the light of the sun and being designed to reflect that light into the great expanse of the universe and onto the earth. Imagine circling forever around those who need you to inspire them. Imagine your view and your position of being between the sun and the earth. See your position in the galaxy.

Lastly, stand on a hill, and plug into a constant source of power. Be the light that can be counted on to guide and give hope. Be the light on the hill! Guide all the travelers to safe harbor. Remember to meditate on the principles of light. Things look different depending on where you are standing. Light makes colors change throughout the day. The intensity and duration of light affect plant growth and our growth. You can be light wherever you are. You can take the role of any light in the heavens, not just the ones we have discussed (they are only metaphors for types of light). You may transform into them as you like and as you need.

I just had a granite countertop installed. In the granite are rivers of crystal, and there are pieces of copper, silver, gold, and mica which can only be seen at night with an overhead light. During the day, they are hidden unless I walk a full circle around the top while tilting my head at an angle. I love that I caught sight of all of those beautiful pieces, and I now view them as excellent reflectors of certain types of light. What kind of light are you? What kind of light do you dream of becoming? With your beautiful brain, imagine all of these types of light; sit and contemplate the smallest nuance of each type, and then experience being a light bearer.

Chapter 11

THE PAST, THE FUTURE AND THE QUANTUM MECHANICS OF NOW

The past will chase you down. It will hunt you like a rabid dog. People will be happy to remind you of your desperate years, your failure to thrive, your time as a zombie. Old friends (pre-bite) will see you, and some will remember how you deserted them for those they considered *losers* and for the *walking dead*. It will be difficult for you to reinvent yourself in their eyes. Your disappearance from active life into the dark net, off the grid, may be a sore wound for old friends. They may decide that there will never be a resurrection of the bridges you burned. Don't talk about your old life; it will give it too much power. Much of what people will say about you will then be true, and much of it will be a fabric of truth and lies woven into a tapestry of support for their conviction of you. You will be on trial...*do not* go to court. Make your life! That will be *evidence* of life after death.

The past will rise up and surprise you. Since you have activated your angels, things might have changed more than you are aware. Maybe you have sent them to repair old hurts and old offenses. Some of your friends, who knew you before you were bitten, will be excited to see you happy and alive. It could be like a dream in which they found their best friend or child. These friends will be eager to love and encourage you. They are the ones who have refused to gossip about you, and when those who wanted to badmouth you "shared," they stood up for you or walked away. You may have never spent much time with these people, but they have the heart of a friend for you. It will surprise you to find out who your friends really are. Those that whisper old truths and lies about you or question your new path are not your friends. They may be like record players that play your parents' old tapes or your own negative self-talk. You may even have picked these friends long ago to reflect or replay negative images of you. Let them go!

The past is a wild horse that requires a saddle and a bridle. Your past may have been wild, rebellious, and really exciting. Or, maybe it was very predictable, safe, and boring. Either way, you will need to identify the indirect path you took from there to here. Something or someone made you hide who you really were and what you really wanted. Did your parents enforce rules and regulations? Did they help you all the way to college and then leave you to your own devices after protecting you from the world? Were you shocked by how easy it was to derail, or was it all a part of your plan? Review your past to search for the footprints of dissatisfaction, unhappiness, broken fences, and broken relationships.

You need a saddle and a bridle because you may not want to discard the old horse, but rather tame it. You will miss the lesson if you only reflect on the "wild" you. From every mistake and every success, you have learned much about yourself and others. Retain these lessons. Reflect on everything, and write down what you learned from walking through the past. Reveal the truths you learned during your pre-bite and bite phases. Saddling represents riding this knowledge, the solid beast of desire and progression. Bridling means that you harness the force and retain this knowledge to direct and use it for new purposes. You can use misspent passions to move forward, then keep the lessons.

The past is a sling shot that catapults you forward. Now you understand that certain behaviors were not useful, and all of the distractions of your young life have kept you from fulfilling your dreams. Now, can you imagine capturing all that motion and misspent energy to catapult you forward? It is like discovering the light bulb. Edison said he did not fail a thousand times; he just found a thousand ways not to make a lightbulb. If you make a thousand missteps, then you just might be a thousand steps closer to your goals. What you thought was wasted—your past—is now power, clarity, and direction, if viewed as a training ground for your future.

Riding the horse back, to use resources from the past, is a useful strategy. Examine all the old wounds, and determine what beliefs you have and where they came from. Excavate old audio/visual cues from experiences that you were too young to process. What beliefs did you develop from the misinterpretation of what you heard, saw, or felt? Doing this will set you free from damaging illusions.

For example, I had one client who was excellent in all her studies except math. She had postponed taking the subject because she was convinced that she was bad at math. When I helped her remember the first time that she knew she was bad at math, it was when she was five. Her grandmother was in the hospital when her aunt came to see her. She watched and listened to her grandmother and her aunt's conversation. Her grandmother asked her aunt, "How is school?" Her aunt replied, "Okay, but math is kicking my butt." Her grandmother said, "Well, none of us were ever good at math." That was one of the last things she ever heard her grandmother say. The message came in early, during a very emotional event. This was a generalization and misinterpretation of what she heard. Her young mind heard that if she wanted to belong to her grandmother's family; if she wanted to belong to the "we," she had to be "bad" at math. Her young mind cemented the relationship with math by walling off her understanding so she could belong to the family of "we."

Once we discussed the incident to determine what Grandma was really trying to say and what Auntie was really trying to say, she realized that none of it was meant or directed towards her. She could understand that it was simply "small talk." She was able to see that her grandmother would have never wanted her to believe that she was not good at a subject and that her Auntie's "butt" was not being kicked at all. I placed her on a virtual timeline. As we stepped off the timeline, I asked her if her aunt had learned what she needed to learn. Had she herself learned enough math to get into college? I asked her if there were study habits that she knew that helped her to get A's in all her other classes.

As she answered the questions, she was able to provide her young, five-year-old, self with future knowledge that her aunt would learn math and graduate college and go on to use math in her field. She was able to see that she got straight A's in all her other subjects, so she could learn math as well. She went from a 60 percent after 5 weeks in her first college math class to her first A on a math test, in only five days, after her session. She earned a 94 percent on her test just by removing her belief that she was "bad at math." She learned that everything she had ever learned about math was in her brain waiting to be accessed. Her early childhood auditory experience had occurred during a very emotional and turbulent family crisis, which embedded it even deeper into her psyche, causing her to erect a wall between herself and math.

There are several other ways that you can go back to tame all that you thought unmanageable, to help propel you to the future. Everything you have ever learned can be reframed and restructured to create new beliefs that can advance you towards your present goals. You can rewrite the stories to give each of the characters whatever they need to be more resourceful. You can rewrite your story, and play it forward and backward. You can step into it wherever you want to re-experience it in a new way. You can erase all of the cellular memory of any injury event so that you can be free of all the trauma and drama of your past, while using all of the learning to keep the depth of character you will need to get where you are going. By going back through a painful experience and changing what you did just before the event, you will signal the brain that the event never happened. It takes quite a few times through the *reimagining process* to make your brain erase all of the cellular memory, but this method can and does change everything.

Whatever you do with your past, your future is waiting for you. If you have prepared yourself by doing all that you were directed to do prior to this, you are ready to imagine your future. In previous chapters, we talked about how to discover your passion, and you were directed to study those in your field. If you found the image of your passionate and successful self, then keep the image. Once you have the image in your mind's eye then detail it with as much 3-D layering of information as you can discover. This is the key to holding that image. It is like an antenna that keeps the channel set on the purest image. The more detail and the more pixels, the better the picture. Begin by dialing in. When the eye doctors check your eyesight, they ask you which lens is better. This or that? Then, he has you look at another set and ask the same questions. You need to do the same thing: keep adjusting the picture until you get it perfectly dialed in and clear. Then, visit that picture ten times a day for the first month. It will fuel your actions. Look way out into the one-year, two-year, and five-year pictures to see what is different. Keep in mind that the long-term goal is met by consistently meeting short-term goals.

You rewrote your story and then reframed it using the instructions of previous chapters. If there are any parts left that still have the power to hurt you, to slow you down, or to haunt you, then it is time to change this Now. Using a theater technique (10) to rewind the film of your life and change all of the parts and characters that need to be changed will help you live your best life Now. YOU can change your character to have more truth, compassion, mercy, and love. You can edit "you" to behave in ways that would have completely changed your future. Before you rewrite, be sure to capture all you learned about yourself and others. Work to retain the knowledge of the representation of you. Replay the new film ten times with the new and better outcomes. Then, see how you feel about your life.

The Quantum Mechanics of NOW is part of the title of this chapter but you need to know- **"What's Special About Quantum Physics?"** In the realm of quantum physics, observing something actually influences the physical processes taking place. Light waves act like particles, and particles act like waves (called wave particle duality). Matter can go from one spot to another without moving through the intervening space (called *quantum tunneling*). Information moves instantly across vast distances. In fact, in quantum mechanics, we discover that the entire universe is actually a series of probabilities. Taken from Nova.PBS (2008-2015)

What does this mean for you? This is the science that explains why returning to your past and stepping away from the timeline to observe what is happening, changes the events of the past! Then, getting back onto your timeline to walk forward to the present will change the **you** that you are NOW and therefore the future as well. Changing as much or as little as is needed, makes huge differences in the outcomes. I say "outcomes" because there is a series of probabilities. The theories are complex, but essentially, whatever you observe is changed just by your observations. So, changing your observation (your mind about what will be seen) and then observing the event actually changes the event (this is the particle theory). If the event did affect you, the new observation changes the new you.

This may seem somewhat confusing. Here is your takeaway: if you want to change something, use super focus. While in that waking state of a trance, see it change, and move it. Move it to the corner of the page, make it small, put it in a frame, change the color to grey and white, change all the possible outcomes that you can imagine and then experience it minimized or completely changed into the best scenario. How you feel about the event and the outcomes will have been altered in a credible way. It really works. This proves how powerful you were made to be. It is time to use that power to change your mind and change your life!

"NOW" is the most powerful word in the English language! Now you can see your past, and now you can envision your future. From the place called "Now," you can Quantum jump to any space you want without tunneling through irrelevant time and space. Now can be any point in time that you want to focus on, and in that now, you can change the lines of time as it relates to you. Now you can choose who you are, and now you can choose what is real and what was a probability that you decided to leave unrealized. Now you can be wherever and whatever you can see, in any time or space you want to be. Be HERE NOW: it is the greatest and most powerful space to occupy. Do not waste Now, it is a currency that is more valuable than particles of gold and silver. It is a magical place between the past and the future where we can hope all things, imagine all things and be all that was and all that will be-NOW!

CHAPTER 12

SPEAKING THE WORLD INTO BEING

"In the beginning was the Word and the Word was with God and the Word was God" (1 John 1:1 NIV). God spoke the world into being. The first name of God was unspeakable because it was breathed. "Yahweh" means the breath of God. If you say it, you should breathe in "Yah" and breathe out "Weh" because to speak it, you must take the breath. Your first breath was at birth, and then you cried. That was your first expression! Without breath, there is no life. This is a powerful metaphor for what we are meant to do: speak or breathe our world into being. The actual Jewish spelling is Yawe.

Many scholars and early mystics have claimed that what scientists call the Big Bang, or the creation of the universe, was God speaking it into being. Early Jewish mystics said that He built the universe with the Hebrew Aleph-Beit: "As a carpenter employs tools to build a home, so G-d utilized the twenty-two letters of the Hebrew Alphabet to form heaven and earth" (Rav Ruskin). In <u>Letters of Light: A Journey Through Hebrew The Alphabet,</u> *(17)* it says that God honed the letters and then built the universe out of the letters when he spoke them into being.

In another book by Rav Berg, The 72 Names of Gd (18) (God is spelled Gd by Rabbis) he explained that the letters are evident in Quantum Mechanics. The frequency in each letter brings about a power source. Putting the letters together brings their power and meaning to each three letter name. For example, MEM means water, but not just water, rather all of properties that water possesses. Rav Berg says in *The 72 Names of Gd* that these names are like appliances that when spoken are plugged into the power source of Gd (18). The Hebrew letters bring all of the letters' qualities, characteristics, and meanings to the name they form. Each letter is like a pictograph of a concept that expresses a full vision of its meaning.

Using your tongue to speak your world into being is not only truth, but it is also reflective of who you are. You were breathed into being as His representation on earth. You are to mirror the Father. But, we fell asleep to the power and to our inheritance. What have you been speaking? Where did you get the thought that formed the speech? Before you speak-think through this–Proverbs 18:21 KJV "Death and life are in the power of the tongue: and they that love it shall eat the fruit thereof."

The tongue is a monster to be tamed. It has been trained by your auditory tapes, culture, thoughts, and beliefs. It can be an excavator, a stealth bomber, a crane, or a box of TNT. It can drip honey or toxins. It can destroy or create; it is up to you. God used his voice to say, "Let there be light!" Managing your thought life and then using your tongue to bless yourself and others is a good place to start. Speaking "I Am" messages (as discussed in chapter

8 of this book) is another way to use this powerful organ. In *The Three-in-One Concise Bible Reference Companion* by Thomas Nelson Publishers(19), there are two pages describing what the tongue can do. If you are older than six years old, you are well aware of the power of the tongue. Some people's words may be burning in your mind right now. It is time to erase old tapes and replace them with a more beautiful truth. Speaking blessings over your life, your friends, your children, and your spouse will absolutely change your life.

Here, I remind you of Dr. Caroline Leaf's book *21 Day Detox for the Brain*.(20) In her book, she said that repeating a new truth or belief for seven minutes a day will make new neuro-pathways. Doing this for 21 days will create a new belief that will be cemented into you. These new thoughts that create new beliefs will create completely new behaviors. Self-destructive behaviors melt away, and your "I am" and "I can" messages will take root.

Which comes first: a thought or your words? Some people say, "they speak before they think." That is from old programming. Needing to recoil and respond with a strike force has come from needing to protect yourself. You may have learned to do this in a place of physical violence. But, I will tell you, words can be just as deadly a blow. It just takes longer to kill someone with words. Destructive, hateful words have been lying under the surface ready to spring out to strike because of the years of being backed into a corner or feeling bullied. Maybe they were used as effective ways to keep people away by building a wall. Sarcasm is a mixture of self-hate and disdain for the things around you. If words have been used to demean, deter, and destroy your character, then you are more likely to become an expert at this method of defense.

It is NOW that you go up to the control tower of your brain and set the response codes to new reaction phrases. Instead of "you are a fool" or "you are stupid," in response to others' beliefs, reprogram your brain with the phrases "tell me more" and "I don't think I understand." Refuse judgment for it will always be on you. Judgment is an anchor and a chain which is an unintended consequence. Instead, program your beliefs to remind you that everyone has difficulties communicating their needs to be significant or to be right. You can be right, but it is a lonely place to be. It is much better to engage in understanding that from all backgrounds, there are sets of life experiences that are not like yours. Remind yourself that they are speaking from that place, and it is not a personal attack on you. Always asking to hear more, lowers their defenses, so that they feel heard or understood. You may never agree with them, but you can understand better. Seek to find things about them and their ideas that are useful or can be a common ground for respect. Snapping and snarling do not create a welcoming environment, but the person doing the snapping may be the one who most needs someone to finally hear them out.

Of course, this does not work with people who have mental health problems or narcissistic or sociopathic tendencies. Disengage, and save your empathy for those who are lost in the floundering social morays of our culture and for yourself. If you have been a victim of bullying, you will need to rebuild your views and replace the old tapes even more than those who are simply affected by culture. But, don't give up on making the changes and on growing your desire to wake up to your passion. Remember, it only requires seven minutes a day for 21 days!

Once you have changed your thoughts, speaking the new truth is vital. See it; say it; write it; hear it; and then do it. Using your visual, auditory, kinesthetic, gustatory, and olfactory senses, explore your new truth. Make that your speech. Here is an example: "I am a writer. My words are clear; my words make word pictures; my words are beautiful to the ears; my words are like warm water on the skin; my words are a fresh breath on the faces of those who hear them; and my words are a fragrant flower that rises itself to the sun and emits the sweet smell that brings the hummingbirds to move my petals. My words uplift and carry the fragrance on the wind to inspire others. My words are a solid body of strength that form a shelter and a safe place." Okay, these are things I say to myself about what I want my words to do and be. You may want to say "I Am" messages over your passions.

Auditory memories can be building blocks or obstacles to learning. What you hear can be extremely damaging to your psyche and to your soul. Your mind may run ahead saying, "What did they mean by that?" As a result, you may miss the rest of the story. If you are an auditory learner, you will not learn well from what you see or read unless you give it a voice by reading it aloud. If this is you, then you may remember everything you ever heard. You may be a musician because words are music and frequencies to you that are beautiful in note or word forms. You may find ways to express yourself in this way. You also may need to be quiet to hear the world around you.

You also might be quite wounded. In this world where everything is text or tweets, short abbreviations of thoughts, you may feel quite misunderstood. You might be misunderstanding others and disengaging from social media. If you cannot hear the tone and intonation to give the words life, color, and meaning, it can be a confusing way for an auditory learner to communicate. You may prefer actual telephone conversations. Hearing a voice, trees rustling, wind moving, and all the cacophony of sounds of the world's organisms is pure joy to you. As an auditory learner, words hold tremendous value for you. You are less likely to speak, but when you do, people listen. It is always obvious that you have been listening with your entire being. You make a very special kind of friend, and you wound quite easily, so it is most important for you to say, "Tell me more." It is also important to develop a framework for determining how to know if what you hear is true.

Using an auditory memory to create is an extraordinary technique to embed thoughts. Making tapes of your "I Am" messages and then playing them over and over using hypnotic trance language to reach a deeper level of consciousness is a powerful way to make and maintain changes. Most Apple products have a garage band on them, and you can use it to make a CD message for yourself. Create an in-depth six-minute vocal recording on a loop of your "I Am" messages, and listen to them when you walk, sleep, or drive. If you use it to drive, be sure to embed a message reminding you to be fully aware of all of your surroundings while learning. Embed a message that communicates that all of your conscious attention is focused on your tasks, while your subconscious mind is absorbing your beliefs and "I Am" messages at the deepest level.

Harnessing the power of the tongue, the ears, and physical body to create your experiences and embed your new beliefs will require repetition and cellular memory. You will be developing new neuro-pathways, which is similar to building roads. You will have to plow, grade, and blast a path through difficult terrain. You will have to smooth out the edges. You will have to pave it so that you can quickly and easily get where you are going. To go further, you will continue to improve the early road to expand and extend. It will require maintenance.

Here is an example for those of you just beginning. This set of "I Am" messages will allow your subconscious to develop rich content regarding your gifts and purpose. Make a recording of these:

I rise each morning to a new day.

Each morning I am strong, awake, and alive!

I wake excited to see what the day will bring.

I stand strong, flexible, whole, and healthy.

I know that good things will happen to me today.

I trust that life is good and that God has plans to prosper me and not to harm me.

The deeper I sleep, the more I know about my talents and gifts!

Each morning, I wake with new details about my gifts that make me even more passionate about sharing them.

I receive new ideas for new ways to share my unique gifts.

I awake with intuition about who can help me learn more about my gifts and talents.

I meet people who inspire me every day.

I look forward each day to the surprises and delights that await my eyes and ears.

Each day, I become stronger, kinder, and more loving.

I quickly and easily learn everything I need to for my passionate purpose.

Every day, I experience great favor from those around me.

My angels make a path for me and speak into the ears of those who can give me favor.

People naturally want to help me. I am enjoyed by those around me, and I enjoy those that I meet.

I see clearly the divine spark in each human being, and I am   excited to know more.

I sleep soundly. I wake brightly. I grow more intuitive.

I am grateful for my brain, heart, and body. I am grateful for my soul.

I am filled with divine light and fire.

After hearing this a couple of hundred times, you may want to lay this down under your favorite song and let the message go subliminal (garage band). Your subconscious mind will hear all of your messages, while your conscious mind sings along with your favorite album. You can do the same thing using your core values, using the "I believe" messages. Choosing all the beliefs that you want to believe, all of the truths that you want to be true, all of your mission statements, and all of your passionate purpose statements, you can uniquely design your own statements and play them over and over. We are what we say. So practice your voiceover as well as your auditory learning. If you are kinesthetic, you can write and rewrite these messages as well as play games with them. A powerful tool is the Mind's Eyeglasses. They have light and color flashes that sync your brain with a frequency of learning. They have different programs for sleep or deep trance states. While in that state, you can instill your learning deep into your psyche by playing your messages with the glasses on. This is a great way to dive beyond your conscious guards that may be producing negative self-talk while listening to positive messages.

You may also not trust your own voice, so if you still have behaviors that are not in alignment with your messages, you can change the voice by having someone else, such as a maternal or paternal voice, read your messages. It may be helpful to listen to several different voices as verification that others believe this. The power of others' beliefs may be quite important to you, and rather than fighting that, use it to change what you want. We are complicated creatures, and we have parts of ourselves that hate change that we will need to battle. We have to use all strategies possible to integrate ourselves and allow for accordance.

You have done the work. You have embedded your beliefs and reframed them, resourced them, paraphrased them, listened to them, repeatedly written them, ran over them with heavy duty equipment, played them on a different frequency, said them in the morning and before going to sleep and while walking, driving, and every other possible way. It is time to be what you say! Embody all that you want to be. Know that in every cell of your body, you are changing from what you were to what you want to be. It will not take years, and it will not take decades. You are now a Quantum jumping machine, when you leap into the new you—the data and details will follow in the wave particles. You are reconstituting yourself and re-molecularizing into the new you. Like a broken bone healing within a cast, you may not see the healing, but it is all coming together. Bone glue has reached out for you, and you will be stronger than ever. You will never be the same. What you will be is up to your tongue. Use that sword of truth wisely to create what you believe.

Chapter 13

LOST, FOUND AND GIVEN

You were lost, sick, and broken. You were BITTEN. Your light had grown dim. The culture that lay like a fog over your soul had taken your future in ways that you never expected. Little by little, there was less of YOU. You were disappearing into the fog. Your disappointment and disillusionment did not occur suddenly; it happened one decision at a time, one pass on a decision, one "whatever." Each time you refused to use your voice, your ideas, your passion, or your talents, you handed a bit of your soul away. Your soul is your heart, personality, and mind. Your spirit is something else entirely. But what makes you uniquely different—your talents, desires, purpose, and drive—are all part of your soul. Each step away from your true self was a blow to your body. You took your grief, anger, and apathy and turned it inward. You found yourself broken with pain, sick often, and diagnosed with new disorders never found in the generations before us. You've had restless leg syndrome, Lyme disease, fibromyalgia, or autoimmune diseases that exploded in this generation and became an epidemic. You suffered from either alcohol addiction, drug addiction, depression, bipolar and other personality disorders, or you were just disillusioned.

You were helpless to change; you lacked the will to change and lacked the vision because of your despair. Hopelessness was your new normal. Oh, sure, you had days that were fun, but then you went back to the drudgery of your life. For example: Did you take a vacation, clear your head and heart, only to come back to everything that you hated about your life? The bad thing was that absolutely everything in our culture was feeding all of the above. Our culture has made suicide honorable and respectable. Death by a doctor, suicide by cop—choices, "they" say! That was evil's whisper to show you a way out. I am so glad you did not take that option and that you are still reading. You are loved, important, and valuable. You are necessary, and you have been awakened for battle. Turn off The Walking Dead, Z Nation, and the eleven other occult spinoffs that are new in 2016. More and more of Hollywood is recognizing our cultural draw to the dark side, and they are capitalizing on it and feeding that beast. Turn off all darkness. It leads to death and destruction and does not provide hope.

Love has pursued you. You are reading this because Love has never given up on you. Love has hunted you down with a passion and a purpose to kiss the sleeping beauty—to awaken you. Love has sent people to battle for you and to intervene on your behalf through prayer and supplication. People you don't even know have prayed for you. As I wrote this book, I prayed for you and wept for you. Each person is important to the Passion Play. There are thousands all over the world who are praying for the lost, the lonely, and the disenfranchised. Prayer warriors, priests, nuns, school teachers, pastors, elders, moms, dads, and grandparents are praying for intervention on your behalf. There are moments you may have felt divine peace surround you during your life. Surprising moments of delight were ordained for you. You are a work in progress, and God is the Author and Finisher of our hope and our lives. Have faith that He is with you and leading you all the days of your life.

Throughout this time of healing, you have felt yourself take back control of your body and your mind. You have learned to feed it faith, hope and love. You have been nurtured back to health. Not there yet? Okay, do a physical check, and you will see that you are better than when you began. It is like a broken bone mending; you may not see the evidence unless you take an X-ray, but you can be assured that both pieces of the bone have been reaching out to each other. They will meet and be stronger. Say, "I am better." Say, "Thank you, Lord, that I am being made well." People are coming around speaking health and hope and happiness over your life because it is more infectious than despair. You are giving them hope because you are emerging victorious over the darkness. When you see their hope, it will feed yours. Mirror neurons are at play; be sure to surround yourself with those who will project health, productive activity, positive direction, passion, and purpose.

Like I said, you were hunted down like a child lost in the forest. Angels lined up fingertip to fingertip to walk through the fog together to find you, even if that meant stumbling over you in the dark and taking you by the hand. The dogged pursuit of you has come from the power, passion, and purpose that God has for you. He says that *Love pursues!*

Once, when I was swimming in Hawaii with my niece, a rogue wave washed in ahead of a rip tide. I was up to my knees in water, and she was up to her waist. That wave crashed down on us then spun her into the sand while pulling us out to sea. I dove deeper to find her, but I couldn't. I dove again further out, but the sand was swirling and made it impossible to see. Blindly, I reached around and found the arm of my five-year-old niece. I clung to that tiny hand with the firmest grip of my life. I then planted my feet firmly in the sand and stood up while yanking her up into my arms. She was microseconds from being gone. Later, I found out that she had a spiral break from that pull. I had been so determined that she would not go out to sea that I had used everything in me. God will do no less. You may end up wounded in the rescue. But you will be found! "Now" is a moment that is between the past and the future. You were and you are saved! He breathed new life and new hope into you, and that was the anti-venom you needed.

You have been healed of the delusion that you were dead, that there was no hope. You have awakened to your life and your value. You know that there is a path for you and someone to walk it with you. You have discovered your value in the eyes of love. You now know how important you are and see clearly the value in others as well. Once you thought that nothing you did or could do would really make any difference. Now you see that one small step after another will lead you out of the darkness and into the light. You have begun to trust the process and to wake to new purpose each day.

Through that process, you have reconstructed your core values. You painstakingly looked for the things that you liked, enjoyed, and loved. You ripped things out of magazines and wrote things down that you thought important and meaningful to you. You did the work necessary to build on all that made you unique by thinking about it and giving it detail. You did not simply say, "I enjoy skiing," but expanded on how it made you feel, what you got to see, and what strengths and confidence each detail gave you. You detailed each thought so that you recaptured your light and brought all the lost shards of your soul back to you.

Once you recaptured your lost light, you decided what kind of light you were and how you were going to shine. You made decisions about where and when you would shine your light. You surrounded yourself with people who would breathe into your fire and believe in you. You found your source of fuel to feed your fire and plugged into the divine. Everyone and everything else were only your resources. The Source is enough because when we do not have a friend to encourage, the Source will bring one. When we do not have the funds to go forward with our dreams, the Source has already provided.

You have activated your faith and found mentors in your field, mentors for your spiritual growth, and better friends. Now, you understand that you have a responsibility to do the same—to be a light in the dark. You have placed yourself in the constellations to shine. By giving back the light you absorbed and watching life grow and thrive in front of your very eyes, by your willingness to do the hard work, you have become a resource for someone else. Being part of something bigger than yourself has only made you stronger and more resilient to battle the forces of darkness.

By traveling back in time to change your story, by using the auditory and visual reconstructions, you learned that changing your perspective has changed everything. By rewriting your story and placing more resources along the path to your future, you have made evidence of faith. Every day you will find that your angels have provided resources along your path. Those resources are proof of how faithful God has been to complete and support His work in you. Taking control of the story that God had in store for you, and using all of the gifts and talents that He gave to you, have changed your mind, your beliefs, and your future.

While working through the directives of this book, you began to harness the quantum mechanics of "Now." You used your tongue to speak your world into being. Using your words to increase your passion and your purpose, you have found the secret and the key to the Kingdom of Heaven. The Kingdom of Heaven is within you; knock and the door will be opened. Praise Him, and Heaven will rain blessings over you. Be like the Father, who spoke the universe, and then "it was." Like Him, say, "Let there be Light." Be with the creator, and be co-creator of the New Jerusalem by giving Him your will. You can never out give God. When you think you have given everything, you will be given more than you ever thought or imagined: "Ear hath not heard nor eye has seen all that I have in store for you" (1 Corinthians 2:9 KJV.) With passion, every day, rise and say, "You better run, evil. I am up and running with my angels to do battle for my soul, this earth, and the lives to come!

Chapter 14

SITTING IN HOLINESS, RESTING IN MERCY

When God finished the world, He rested. He gave us this example that after we work hard to create our new world we will need to rest. We will need to give ourselves permission to just "be." We live in a culture that feeds us several mixed messages: Rest more! Work Harder! Don't overthink it! Take time to self-examine! Take care of you! You are the most important person! Selfies are everywhere. The focus on "self" has taken us further away from ourselves than we have ever been because we are looking to the wrong places for our validation and worth. It is time to set all of that aside, to really learn how to rest and how to reflect. What is rest: Hebrews 4:1 (KJV) states "enter into my rest." The meaning here is to trust and to have faith that the world will go on without your efforts while you sleep, read, fish, or just sit on a rock and listen to the birds. Restore your soul with the beauty that surrounds you. If you live in a concrete jungle, you may have to visit nature, but you can also wall yourself off in your house and fill your mind with images that you have seen. Reflect on your day, your efforts, and your outcomes. Think about whether your actions are really aligning with your core values. Psalms

62:1 (KJ21) says "my soul finds rest in God alone." Even God took a day to rest. "Rest" is a key part of "restore." Rest restores our souls, our bodies, and our spirits.

Doing nothing can be more powerful than action! There is a time for action, but people are quite busy and believe that they should never be without something to do. "Do something" is quite frequently a mantra. In this book you have been given many directives. I have given you a large "to do list" that you may need to take quite a bit of time doing. It is important to enter into rest every seven days for a complete day of "rest." When I enter into rest, which has been a very difficult task for me, I imagine laying all of my concerns, ideas, problems, tasks, and conflicts at my Father's feet. I choose a visual hammock to climb into and just lie there feeling the slight sway. I watch the leaves on the trees above catch and receive the light with each soft sway. I marvel at the light and wind's dance. I completely surrender to being. In that state of being, I focus on just being loved.

It is very difficult in our culture to do nothing because many people view resting as a waste of time. "You can sleep when you're dead" is a commonly used phrase. But, if you will learn to relax into the great void of being, you will be filled because the universe hates a void. In this state, you may hear the voice and sentiment of God. Quieting the mind and the body makes us acutely aware of even the air on our skin. Entering into being present, relaxed, and clear, gives us renewed vigor for all the tasks we choose. If you make time for this practice, it will make a difference in your breathing and your stress level. It will create a space that allows you to experience Holiness.

What is Holiness? It is divine perfection, purity, and

peace. It is a righteousness unattainable by any of us through our works but attainable through the brilliant life of the Triune God. "Holy! Holy! Holy!" is the song of angels, and it is the praise of God in three persons: God the father, God the son, and God the Holy Spirit. When we move away from all the noise and focus on the One in us who is Holy, He will point us to the Father and the Son and will guide us on our path. In Hebrews 10:16(NIV), the Holy Spirit testifies to us about this: "This is the covenant I will make with them after a time, says the Lord. I will put my laws in their hearts and I will write them on their minds. Their sins and lawless acts I will remember no more. And where they have been forgiven, there is no longer any sacrifice for sin." It is time to rest in His love. This is more powerful than taking any action toward goals, dreams, or intuitions.

When you lay down your cares, be sure you take all of your judgments to the altar. Be totally set free from these mental arguments. "For we wrestle not against flesh and blood but against principalities." (Ephesians 6:12 KJV) You cannot do in the flesh what spirits can do in the spiritual realms and heavenly places. Leave your battles with your angels and with your God. He has your back. Have faith that He will make all things new again. Forgive yourself and others to set yourself free. Imagine all the people that you have been holding thoughts against, and imagine that every thought connects you to that person or persons by a ball and chain. Unlock the chains or cut yourself free of those thoughts and soar above trials and tribulations by taking on the spirit of joy: "The joy of the Lord is my Salvation." (Nehemiah 8:10 NIV)

When negative thoughts come to your mind, practice "thought interrupt," which is used by mind management and cognitive behavioral therapists (the first one being Jesus, then Dr. Caroline Leaf, Mark and Magali Peycha, Bennett Stellar, and others). Try new thoughts to place into your negative thought patterns. Soon, your strategies will be your first thoughts. This verse offers the best instruction on this matter: "Do not be anxious about anything but in every situation by prayer and petition, with thanksgiving, present your request to God. And the peace of God which transcends all understanding will guard your hearts and minds in Christ Jesus. Finally, brothers and sisters, whatever is true, whatever is noble, whatever is right, whatever is pure, whatever is lovely, whatever is admirable, if anything is excellent or praiseworthy, think about such things." (Philippians 4:6-8 NIV)

A few days after writing the last two lines above, I was watching a Ron Carpenter sermon when I heard a woman say that she had an extremely fearful child who was diagnosed with a most severe case of Obsessive Compulsive Disorder (OCD). She went on to say how many doctors they had been to and how crippled he was with anxiety. He was only seven years old when it began. Finally, after a few years, God spoke to her and told her to ask her son some questions and have him write down the answers. So she asked her son, "What is true?" He told her, "You and Dad and our home are true." She asked, "What else do you know to be true?" They wrote his answers down together. She went on to ask, "What is noble?" Then they wrote that answer down. Based on the verse in the previous paragraph, you see where these questions came from. The next questions that she asked, and the answers they wrote, were about things that were right and pure, lovely, admirable, excellent, and praiseworthy. When they were finished, they printed the answers and then placed them all over the house to remind him what to "think on" when he became afraid. Substituting these thoughts is much more effective than doing any other "thought interrupt." Her son was totally cured. The doctors and counselors thought he would never go to public school or be able to work, but he went to school after practicing his new way of thinking. He is even in college today! Practicing these thoughts and meditation on the Holiness of God will help prepare you for all God has in store for you.

Your spirit, your conscious mind, and your light affect the earth. Listening to the Holy Spirit and learning to control your mind will make your light shine brightly to all who come into contact with you. Joy and freedom come with knowing all of the things that you have learned. Meditation, discipline, and perseverance were required to find the shards of light that had been broken. Now that you have recreated your passionate purpose, you have been given responsibilities. Now that you know, you will have to share. Your light affects the world! There are so many lost souls who just need your smile to continue. They may just need to be seen by you, to make a momentary connection. Many people on the street say, "I feel like I am invisible."

If you are in a good place, it might be time to be the moon and reflect the light of the Savior. Reflect his mercy, love, and goodness. Offer a cup of cold water, beam His love out into the community, and live the story He gave you. To do this, you must ask yourself, "Who am I reflecting right now?" It can be quite easy to be down or hurt and begin to reflect darker pieces of our stories or just darker pieces of our culture. Road rage, reactions to being insulted or ignored, disappointments, failures, and heartbreak can lead us to a path down a hill into the valleys where we can't get a good signal. When this happens, be sure to quickly turn to your "I Am" messages to get back onto the path of light. Immersing yourself into the testaments and the scriptures of healing and forgiveness will start to infill you with love. The Philippians 4:6-8(NIV) exercise will also deeply connect you with what you value. This requires adjusting your antennae for better reception and keeping yourself resourceful.

While you are reminding yourself that you are a child of God, a human, do not forget that man was placed in the garden. The garden is on Earth. He asked Adam to name all the plants and animals that He created. He gave you "the leaves of the tree for the healing of the nations" (Revelation 22:2 NIV). You can experience healing by going out into the natural world and re-experiencing creation. Learn the names of the trees and the medicines that can be created from those trees. Observing wildlife in nature can be an awe-inspiring experience. Seeing the beautiful creatures that God made for our enjoyment restores our souls. Beauty is a great healer. Nature is a source of beauty. But remember, nature and the earth are resources, and the maker is the Source and the One to whom we give the "glory".

Water is one of the greatest and most beautiful resources of the universe. Where there is water, there is life. Jesus said to the woman at the well, "Everyone who drinks of this water will be thirsty again but whoever drinks of the water that I will give him will never be thirsty again" (John 4:13-14 NJV). Most of life has a density made mostly of water. We are arguably over ninety percent water. Water affects us, and we have a tremendous effect on water. Dr. Emoto's <u>Messages from the Water</u> includes a scientific examination of the power of words over water. Our prayers and gratitude change large and small bodies of water. We are "actors" on water; what we think, pray or do changes water and water changes everything. This is an extreme resource that we can use to change the earth, to change people, and to impact all life. The water, earth, and sky have had a symbiotic relationship from the moment God spoke the world into being. Genesis 1:6 (NLT) states "and God said 'Let there be an expanse between the waters to separate water from water. So God made the expanse and separated the water under the expanse from the water above it and it was so. God called the expanse 'sky'. Genesis 1:9 (NLT) says: "let the water under the sky be gathered to one place and let the dry ground appear."

The waters in the heavens rain down onto the earth and separate into streams, rivers, and lakes. The waters undergo the evaporation process and return to the sky and again to the earth, which is a part of the eco-system of every living thing. A man drinks water, is water, returns water to the earth, and when he dies, returns as ashes back to earth: as our eulogists say "ashes to ashes and dust to dust". You have a tremendous impact as a child of God, to save water, clean water, send water, create water, and pray for water. Bring everything back into focus that you have learned. There are laws of God that are in play, and they apply to us all.

During this period of gathering your light and understanding who you are and what you can do with the things of God and the God-particles in you, you have automatically become more of who you were created to be. You have found your light, the Source of light, and the Holy Spirit living in you, and you have learned how to meditate and pray the prayers of the Essenes, the Living Word. Now, spend time in prayer mending your heart, your lungs, and your brain. Examine the tears that have accumulated each day as slings and arrows have tried to penetrate your armor, and the ethereal fabric of your spirit and soul, as well as the physical body. Each day, spend time with God to turn from the world and to receive the Holiness of God in Communion. Breathe the light and love of God into your lungs, and then feel the oxygen flow to all of your organs and cells of your body. Breathe out all of the impurities that your body absorbed in these cleansing breaths. Do this for several breaths until you feel that the air you are expelling is purified. Then, breathe into the world all the love, perfection, and holiness that you can envision while being one with the Divine Creator as He cleanses the world. Rest in His mercy.

You are a beautiful message sent by God to this planet. Your divine spark was torn from Him during the Big Bang when he first spoke the world into being. He planned for you to come here to commune with him and to be a keeper of His plan and message. You have been called to a divine and passionate purpose. He is calling everyone to return to His plan and the Way. His plan is for us to be light, water, hope, mercy, truth, charity, and love on this earth. We are his hands and heart. He came to dwell with us and in us so that we might do miracles in His name. As His children, we are the loved, the healed, and the righteousness of God here on earth. We are the message! We are here to offer what we have received, and then He will pour into our hearts and minds more than we can ever fully understand. For it is written, "Ear hath not heard, nor eye have seen, the things I have in store for you!"(1 Corinthians 2:9 NIV) Claim your passionate purpose, and share all that you are with the world. We need you! Be the message and the messenger, then **rest!**

REFERENCES CITED

(1) The Walking Dead: Kirkman, Robert, Charles Adlard, Tony Moore, Tom Luse, Frank Darabont, Michelle MacLaren, Charles H. Eglee, Jack LoGiudice, Gwyneth Horder-Payton, Johan Renck, Glen Mazzara, Ernest R. Dickerson, Adam Fierro, Guy Ferland, Andrew Lincoln, Jon Bernthal, Laurie Holden, Sarah W. Callies, Steven Yeun, Jeffrey DeMunn, Chandler Riggs, Gregory Nicotero, Howard Berger, David Boyd, Rohn Schmidt, Julius Ramsay, Hunter M. Via, Sidney Wolinsky, and Bear McCreary. The Walking Dead: The Complete First Season. Beverly Hills, Calif: Anchor Bay Entertainment, 2010.

(2) Z Nation is an American horror-comedy-drama/post-apocalyptic television series that airs on Syfy, created by Karl Schaefer and Craig Engler, and produced by The Asylum. DireThe first season of 13 episodes premiered on September 12, 2014.first season of 13 episodes premiered on September 12, 2014: Netflix

(3)The Zombie Apocalypse Production company(s), Asylum. Release. Original network, Syfy. Original October 29, 2011 (2011-10-29). Zombie Apocalypse (or 2012: Zombie Apocalypse) is a film by Syfy and The Asylum starring ... Directed by, Nick Lyon ...

(4) Golems: Rabbi Dr. Louis Jacobs (1920-2006) was a

Masorti rabbi, the first leader of Masorti Judaism (also known as Conservative Judaism) in the United Kingdom, and a leading writer and thinker on Judaism.

(5) Budge, E. A. Wallis. The Egyptian Book of the Dead. London: Cassell, 2001. Print.

(6) Sean of the Dead: Universal Pictures, Studio Canal and Working Title Films present a WT2 production in association with Big Talk Productions produced in association with Inside Track 2, LLP ; produced by Nira Park ; written by Simon Pegg and Edgar Wright ; directed by Edgar Wright. Shaun of the Dead. Universal City, CA :Rogue Pictures : Universal Studios Home Entertainment, 2007. Print

(7)The Empathic Brain by Christian Keysers, 2011 Copyright 2011

8) Switch On Your Brain: The Key to Peak Happiness, Thinking, and Health by Leaf, Dr. Caroline (August 4, 2015) Paperback 1700 by Dr. Caroline Leaf

9) 10 Ways Dance Strengthens the Brain by Ruth Bucznsky, Ph.D. 2015

10) Robbins-Madanes Training | RMTCenter. (n.d.). Retrieved August 7, 2016, from http://rmtcenter.com/

11) Mark and Magali Peysha, Strategic Intervention Handbook: How to quickly produce profound change in yourself and others Kindle Edition. (n.d.). Retrieved August 07, 2016, from https://www.amazon.co.uk/Strategic-Intervention-Handbook-profound-yourself-ebook/dp/B00J15H0A

12) Neruo-lingquistic Programing by Richard Bandler – See Bibliography list for works by:

13) Erickson, M. H., & Rosen, S. (1982). My voice will go with you: The teaching tales of Milton H. Erickson, M.D. New York: Norton.

14) Bennett Stellar University, Michael Bennett, www.imagineit.org

15) Space Odyssey: Kubrick, Stanley, and Arthur C. Clarke. 2001: A Space Odyssey. United States: Metro-Goldwyn-Mayer Corp, 1968.

16) Theater Technique taught to me at Bennett Stellar University, By Michael Bennett, BennettStellar University @ imagineit.org Originally taught as a Nlp Technique from Richard Bandler, co-founder with John of Neuro Linquistic programing. Richard Bandler advanced it from Milton Erickson's Rewind Hypnotic Language pattern techniques. Complete book lists in Bibliography.

17) Letters Of Light: A Mystical Journey Through The Hebrew Alphabet , 1990 by Rabbi Aaron L. Raskin.

18) The 72 Names of Gd: Technology for the Soul, by Yehuda Berg, published by The Kabbalah Center, 2004

19) The Three-in-One Concise Bible Reference Companion by Thomas Nelson Publishers. 1982

2o) 21 Day Detox for the Brain, by Dr. Caroline Leaf, August 5 2015.

21) Messages from the Water, by Dr. Masaru Emoto, 2001

Admin

Home
Table of Contents
Pressbooks.com: Simple Book Production

BODY AND MIND EXTENDED BIBLIOGRAPHY

References

Bandler, R., Andreas, S., & Andreas, C. (1985). Using your brain–for a change. Moab, UT: Real People Press.

Bandler, R. (2008). Richard Bandler's guide to trance-formation: How to harness the power of hypnosis to ignite effortless and lasting change. Deerfield Beach, FL: Health Communications.

Brennan, B. A. (1988). Hands of light: A guide to healing through the human energy field: A new paradigm for the human being in health, relationship, and disease. Toronto: Bantam Books.

Cayce, H. L. (1971). Dreams; the language of the unconscious. Virginia Beach, VA: A.R.E. Press.

Doidge, N. (2007). The brain that changes itself: Stories of personal triumph from the frontiers of brain science. New York: Viking.

Havens, R. A., & Walters, C. (1989). Hypnotherapy scripts: A neo-Ericksonian approach to persuasive healing. New York: Brunner/Mazel.

Horan, P. (1992). Empowerment through Reiki: The path

to personal and global transformation. Wilmot, WI: Lotus Light Publications.

Keysers, C. (2011). The empathic brain: How the discovery of mirror neurons changes our understanding of human nature. Lexington, KY: Social Brain Press.

Kunz, B., & Kunz, K. (2007). Complete reflexology for life. New York, NY: DK. Leaf, C. (n.d.). Switch On Your Brain: The Key to Peak Happiness, Thinking, and Health.

Lundberg, P. (2003). The book of shiatsu: A complete guide to using hand pressure and gentle manipulation to improve your health, vitality, and stamina. New York: Simon & Schuster.

Mlodinow, L. (2012). Subliminal: How your unconscious mind rules your behavior. New York: Pantheon Books.

Paul, N. L. (2005). Reiki for dummies.

Powers, M. (1949). Hypnotism revealed: The Powers technique of hypnotizing and self-hypnosis, including the intriguing chapter, sleep and learn. No.Hollywood, CA: Melvin Powers/Wilshire Book.

Powers, M. (1953). Advanced techniques of hypnosis; a professional hypnotist reveals new procedures for inducing both deep and self hypnosis. Los Angeles: Wilshire Book.

Seth, A., & Bekinschtein, T. (2014). 30-second brain: The 50 most mind-blowing ideas in neuroscience, each explained in half a minute. Sydney: Pier9.

Siegel, D. J. (2007). The mindful brain: Reflection and

attunement in the cultivation of well-being. New York: W.W. Norton.

Tiers, M. (2010). Integrative hypnosis: A comprehensive course in change. United States: CreateSpace.

Vaknin, S. (2010). The big book of NLP expanded: 350 techniques, patterns & strategies of euro linguistic programming. U.S.: Inner PatchPublishing.

Wildwood, C. (1999). Aromatherapy: An introductory guide to essential oils for health and well-being. Shaftesbury: Element.

Young, S. (2004). Break through pain: A step-by-step mindfulness meditation program for transforming chronic and acute pain. Boulder, CO: Sounds True.

APA formatting by BibMe.org.

SPIRIT EXTENDED BIBLIOGRAPHY

Aldana, J. (1998). The 15-minute miracle revealed. Los Gatos, CA: Inner Wisdom Publications.

Anderson, N. T. (1990). Victory over the darkness: Realizing the power of your identity in Christ. Ventura, CA: Regal Books.

Bender, S. (1995). Everyday sacred: A woman's journey home. San Francisco: HarperSanFrancisco.

Berg, R. (2004). Power of you: Kabbalah wisdom to create the movie of your life. Richmond Hill, NY: Kabbalah.

Berg, Y. (2003). The 72 names of God: Technology for the soul. Los Angeles, CA: Kabbalah Centre.

Bossis, G. (1985). He and I. Sherbrooke, Quebec: Editions Paulines. Braden, G. (2004). The God code: The secret of our past, the promise of our future. Carlsbad, CA: Hay House.

Breathnach, S. B. (1998). Something more: Excavating your authentic self. New York, NY: Warner Books.

Byrne, L. (2008). Angels in my hair: A memoir. New York: Doubleday.

Byrne, R., & Byrne, R. (2006). The secret. New York: Atria Books.

Cameron, K., & Comfort, R. (2006). The way of the Master: Seek and save the lost the way Jesus did, study guide. Bartlesville, OK.: Genesis Publishing Group.

Coello, P. (2004). The alchemist. Bath: Camden.

Cooper, D. A. (1997). God is a verb: Kabbalah and the practice of mysticalJudaism. New York: Riverhead Books.

Copeland, G. (1997). Prayers that avail much. Tulsa, OK: Harrison House.

Cybernetics: Progress of cybernetics ; Proceedings of the 1st international congress sept 1969: Main papers. the meaning of cybernetics. NEURO-and biocybernetics. (1970). London.

Drosnin, M., & ?its?um, D. (1997). The Bible code. New York: Simon & Schuster.

Eldredge, J. (2001). Wild at heart: Discovering the passionate soul of a man. Nashville, TN: T. Nelson.

Emoto, M. (2005). The true power of water: Healing and discovering ourselves. Hillsboro, OR: Beyond Words Pub.

Ferguson, M. (1973). The brain revolution: The frontiers of mind research. NewYork: Taplinger.

Gafni, M. (2001). Soul prints: Your path to fulfillment. New York: Pocket Books.

Graham, B. (1975). Angels: God's secret agents. Garden City, NY: Doubleday.

Graham, F., & Nygren, B. (2002). The name. Nashville, TN: Thomas Nelson.

Hampsch, C. (2007). Opposites attract: Understanding God's design for lasting relationships. Shippensburg, PA: Destiny Image Pubublishers.

Hansen, M. V., & Carson, B. (n.d.). The miracles in you: Recognizing God's amazing work in you and through you.

Harvey, A. (1996). The essential mystics: The soul's journey into truth. Harper SanFrancisco.

Hill, N. (1966). Think and grow rich. No. Hollywood, CA: Melvin Powers, Wilshire Book.

Houston, S. (2006). Invoking Mary Magdalene: Accessing the wisdom of the divine feminine. Boulder, CO: Sounds True.

Kennedy, J. (n.d.). Father, son, and the other one: Experiencing the Holy Spirit as a transforming, empowering reality in your life.

Kula, I., & Loewenthal, L. (2006). Yearnings: Embracing the sacred messiness of life. New York: Hyperion.

Maltz, M. (1960). Psycho-cybernetics: A new way to get more living out of life. Englewood Cliffs, NJ: Prentice-Hall.

Mandino, O. (1968). The greatest salesman in the world. New York: F. Fell.

McDowell, J. (1972). Evidence that demands a verdict: Historical evidences for the Christian faith. San

Bernardino, CA: Campus Crusade for Christ International.

Myss, C. M. (1996). Anatomy of the spirit: The seven stages of power and healing. New York: Harmony Books.

Osteen, J. (2007). Become a better you: 7 keys to improving your life every day. New York: Free Press.

Peth, M. G. (2013). Angel Decoding Secret Keys to Communicating With Your Angels. Balboa Pr.

Petter, F. A., & Yamaguchi, T. (2003). The Hayashi Reiki manual: Traditional

Japanese healing techniques from the founder of the western Reiki system. Twin Lakes, WI: Lotus Press.

Reilly, P. L. (1995). A God who looks like me: Discovering a woman-affirming spirituality. New York: Ballantine Books.

Stone, P. F. (n.d.). The code of the Holy Spirit.

The Bible promise book. (1985). Westwood, NJ: Barbour

Warren, R. (2002). The purpose-driven life: What on earth am I here for? Grand Rapids, MI: Zondervan.

Wholey, D. (1997). The miracle of change: The path to self-discovery and spiritual growth. New York: Pocket Books.

Young, S. (2004). Jesus calling: Enjoying peace in His presence: Devotions for every day of the year.

Nashville: Integrity. Zukav, G. (n.d.). The seat of the soul.

APA formatting by BibMe.org.

SCRIPTURE REFERENCES

Chapter: 1

Psalm 139:16 The Talmud: "Thine eyes did see mine unfinished substance (golmi)."

Chapter: 2

Hebrews 11:1 King James 21st Century, (KJ21) Now faith is the substance of things hoped for, the evidence of things not seen.

Romans 10:17 21st Century King James Version, (KJ21) So then faith cometh by hearing, and hearing by the Word of God.

2 Samuel 6:16 King James Version (KJV)16 And as the ark of the Lord came into the city of David, Michal Saul's daughter looked through a window, and saw king David leaping and dancing before the Lord; and she despised him in her heart.

Psalm 149:33 21st Century King James Version (KJ21) them praise His name in the dance; letthem sing praises unto Him with the timbrel and harp.

Psalm 150:4: KJ21 Praise Him with the timbrel and dance; praise Him with stringed instruments and organs!

Chapter: 3

Ephesians 6:12:21st Century King James Version (KJ21)For we wrestle not against flesh and blood, but against principalities, against powers, against the rulers of the darkness of this world, against spiritual wickedness in high places.

Ephesians 13: 21st Century King James Version (KJ21), take unto you the whole armor of God, that ye may be able to withstand in the evil day and, having done all, to stand. 14 Stand therefore, having your loins girded about with truth, and having on the breastplate of righteousness, 15 and your feet shod with the preparation of the Gospel of peace. 16 Above all, take the shield of faith, wherewith ye shall be able to quench all the fiery darts of the wicked. 17 And take the helmet of salvation and the sword of the Spirit, which is the Word of God, 18 praying always with all prayer and supplication in the Spirit, and watching thereunto with all perseverance and supplication for all saints.

Chapter 4:

Luke 13: 18 21st Century King James Version (KJ21) The Kingdom of Heaven is like a mustard seed.

Mathew 25:34 21st Century King James Version (KJ21)come take your inheritance, the kingdom I prepared for you since the creation of the world.

Luke 17:21: 21st Century King James Version (KJ21) kingdom of God is within you.

Philippians 4:8: 21st Century King James Version (KJ21) whatever is noble, whatever is right, whatever is pure, whatever is lovely, whatever is admirable—if anything is excellent or praiseworthy, think about such things.

Luke 20:17: 21st Century King James Version (KJ21) kingdom of heaven is within you.

Chapter 5:

Ephesians 5:14 21st Century King James Version (KJ21) Wake up O sleeper, Rise from the dead, and Christ will shine on you.

Ps 148.2 New International Version (NIV) Praise him, all his angels; praise him, all his heavenly hosts.

Col 1:16 16 New International Version (NIV) For in him all things were created: things in heaven and on earth, visible and invisible, whether thrones or powers or rulers or authorities; all things have been created through him and for him.

Hebrews 1:14 New International Version (NIV) 14 Are not all angels ministering spirits sent to serve those who will inherit salvation?

Luke 20:36 New International Version (NIV) 36 and they can no longer die; for they are like the angels. They are God's children, since they are children of the resurrection.

Matt 25:31 King James Version (KJV) 31 When the Son of man shall come in his glory, and all the holy angels with him, then shall he sit upon the throne of his glory:

Hebrews 12:22 King James Version (KJV) 22 But ye are come unto mount Sion, and unto the city of the living

God, the heavenly Jerusalem, and to an innumerable company of angels,

2Sam 14:17 King James Version (KJV) 17 Then thine handmaid said, The word of my lord the king shall now be comfortable: for as an angel of God, so is my lord the king to discern good and bad: therefore the Lord thy God will be with thee.

Psalms 103: 20 New Living Translation (NLT) 20 Praise the Lord, you angels, you mighty ones who carry out his plans, listening for each of his commands.

1Timothy 5:21 New Living Translation (NLT) 21 I solemnly command you in the presence of God and Christ Jesus and the highest angels to obey these instructions without taking sides or showing favoritism to anyone.

Jude 8:1 New Living Translation (NLT) 8 In the same way, these people—who claim authority from their dreams—live immoral lives, defy authority, and scoff at supernatural beings.[a]

Matt 22:30 New Living Translation (NLT) 30 For when the dead rise, they will neither marry nor be given in marriage. In this respect they will be like the angels in heaven.

Num 22:22 New Living Translation (NLT) 22 But God was angry that Balaam was going, so he sent the angel of the Lord to stand in the road to block his way. As Balaam and two servants were riding along,

Genesis 6:4:New International Version (NIV) And there was recorded a war in Heaven where Lucifer was cast down and many followed him. KJ21

2Kings 19:35: New International Version (NIV) very night the Lord's messenger went out and killed 185,000 men. KJ21

Matt 26:53 New International Version (NIV) Do you think that I cannot call on my Father and he will at once put at my disposal more than twelve legions of Angels? KJ21

Ephesians 1:20 21st Century King James Version (KJ21) I pray also that the eyes of your heart may be enlightened in order that you may know the hope to which He has called you, the riches of His glorious inheritance in the saints, and His incomparably great power for us who believe. That power is like the working of mighty strength which He exerted in Christ when He raised Him from the dead and seated Him at his right hand in the heavenly realms, far above all rule and authority and power and dominion, and every title that can be given, not only in the present age but also in the one to come. KJ21

Ephesians:11 New International Version (NIV) on the full armor of God, so that you will be able to stand firm against the schemes of the devil. For our struggle is not against flesh and blood, but against the rulers, against the powers, against the world forces of this darkness, against the spiritual forces of wickedness in the heavenly realms.

Hebrews 1:14: New International Version (NIV) Are not all angels ministering spirits sent to serve those who will inherit Salvation?

2nd Kings 19:35: New International Version (NIV) that night the angel of the Lord went out and put to death a hundred and eighty-five thousand men in the Assyrian

Camp. When people got up the next morning, there were all the dead bodies!

Chronicles 4:10: 21st Century King James Version (KJ21) that you would bless me and enlarge my territory! Let your hand be with me and keep me from harm so that I will be free from pain!" God granted him his request.

Psalm 91:11-12 21st Century King James Version (KJ21) for He will command his angels concerning you, to guard you in all your ways; they will lift you up in their hands so that you will not strike your foot against a stone.

James 4:2 21st Century King James Version (KJ21) You have not because you ask not.

Chapter 6:

Old testament is not quoted but stories are referred to in this chapter.

Joshua 5: 6 New International Version (NIV) :6 For the children of Israel walked forty years in the wilderness till all the people who were men of war, who came out of Egypt, were consumed because they obeyed not the voice of the Lord. Unto these the Lord swore that He would not show them the land which the Lord swore unto their fathers that He would give us, a land that floweth with milk and honey.

Joshua 3:14-17 New International Version (NIV) So when the people broke camp to cross the Jordan, the priests carrying the ark of the covenant went ahead of them. Now the Jordan is at flood stage all during harvest. Yet as soon as the priests who carried the ark reached the Jordan and their feet touched the water's edge, the water from upstream stopped flowing. It piled up in a heap a great distance away, at a town called Adam in the vicinity of Zarethan, while the water flowing down to the Sea of the Arabah (the Salt Sea) was completely cut off. So the people crossed over opposite Jericho. The priests who carried the ark of the covenant of the LORD stood firm on dry ground in the middle of the Jordan, while all Israel passed by until the whole nation had completed the crossing on dry ground. NIV

Chapter 8:

John 1:1King James Version (kJV)In the beginning was the word, and the word was with God and the word was God" (John 1). Full scriptures represented in the I am messages:

Ephesians 1:44 21st Century King James Version (KJ21) He hath chosen us in Him before the foundation of the world, that we should be holy and without blame before Him in love.

1 John 5:18: Amplified Bible (AMP)We know [with confidence] that anyone born of God does not habitually sin; but He (Jesus) who was born of God [carefully] keeps and protects him, and the evil one does not touch him.

Colossians 2:10: 21st Century King James Version (KJ21) ye are complete in Him, who is the head of all principality and power,

Matthew 5:14 21st Century King James Version (KJ21) Ye are the light of the world. A city that is set on a hill cannot be hid.

Colossians 3:12 King James Version (KJV)12 Put on

therefore, as the elect of God, holy and beloved, bowels of mercies, kindness, humbleness of mind, meekness, longsuffering;

Psalm 66:8: New Living Translation (NLT) Praise our God, all peoples, let the sound of his praise be heard;

1 Peter 1:23 King James Version (KJV) Being born again, not of corruptible seed, but of incorruptible, by the word of God, which liveth and abideth for ever.

Romans 8:37 King James Version (KJV) Nay, in all these things we are more than conquerors through Him that loved us.

1Peter 2:99 King James Version (KJV) But ye are a chosen generation, a royal priesthood, an holy nation, a peculiar people; that ye should shew forth the praises of him who hath called you out of darkness into his marvelous light;

Romans 6:11 King James Version (KJV) Likewise reckon ye also yourselves to be dead indeed unto sin, but alive unto God through Jesus Christ our Lord.

Chapter 10:

Genesis 1:4 King James Version (KJV)Let there be light' and there was light.

Genesis 1:16 King James Version (KJV) great light to govern the day and a lesser light to govern the night.

Psalm 31:17 New International Version (NIV): Let me not be put to shame, Lord, for I have cried out to you; but let the wicked be put to shame and be silent in the realm of the dead.

Psalm 49:14-15 New International Version (NIV) 14 They are like sheep and are destined to die; death will be their shepherd (but the upright will prevail over them in the morning). Their forms will decay in the grave, far from their princely mansions. 15 But God will redeem me from the realm of the dead;he will surely take me to himself.

Luke 16:29-31 New International Version (NIV) 29 "Abraham replied, 'They have Moses and the Prophets; let them listen to them.' 30 "'No, father Abraham,' he said, 'but if someone from the dead goes to them, they will repent.' 31 "He said to him, 'If they do not listen to Moses and the Prophets, they will not be convinced even if someone rises from the dead."

Chapter 12:

1 John 1:1 New International Version(NIV): In the beginning was the Word and the Word was with God and the Word was God"

Chapter 13:

1Corinthians 2-9 King James Version (KJV) Ear hath not heard nor eye has seen all that I have in store for you.

Chapter 14:

Hebrews 4:1 King James Version (KJV) "enter into my rest."

Hebrews 10:15 New International Version (NIV) This is the covenant I will make with them after a time, says the Lord. I will put my laws in their hearts and I will write them on their minds. Their sins and lawless acts I will remember no more. And where they have been forgiven, there is no longer any sacrifice for sin."

Lamentations 3:23 New International Version (NIV) His mercies are new every morning.

Nehemiah 8:10 New International Version (NIV) The joy of the Lord is my Salvation.

Phil 5-9. King James Version (KJV) Do not be anxious about anything but in every situation by prayer and petition, with thanksgiving present your request to God. And the peace of God which transcends all understanding will guard your hearts and minds in Christ Jesus. Finally, brothers and sisters, whatever is true, whatever is noble, whatever is right, whatever is pure, whatever is lovely, whatever is admirable-if anything is excellent or praiseworthy-think about such things.

Revelation 22:2 King James Version (NJV) he leaves of the tree are for the healing of the nations

John 4:12-15 King James Version (NJV) Everyone who drinks of this water will be thirsty again but whoever drinks of the water that I will give him will never be thirsty again.

Genesis 1:6 King James Version (KJV) Let there be an expanse between the waters to separate water from water. So God made the expanse and separated the water under the expanse from the water above it and it was so. God called the expanse 'sky.'

Genesis 1:9 New Living Translation (NIV) let the water under the sky be gathered to one place and let the dry ground appear. NLT

Corinthians 2:9 New International Version (NIV) "Ear hath not heard, not eye have seen, the things I have in store for you!"

AFTERWARD

AUTHORS NOTE

Dear Reader,

You may have found this book to be a bit overwhelming. There are quite a few directives in each of the chapters to think about. Please go through the book a second or even third time to take notes and to give yourself time to dream and envision your future. We live in a busy world, my prayer for you is the you will carve out time to find your passionate purpose. It will bring so much joy to you and those around you.

A work book will be available as a companion to this book by June of 2018. If you would like further help navigating the pathways to the "new you" please consider attending a future Body, Mind, and Spirit Event, or for personal coaching sessions you can contact me at: skennedysharpe@Gmail.com.

www.ingramcontent.com/pod-product-compliance
Lightning Source LLC
LaVergne TN
LVHW092324080426
835508LV00039B/529